DROPPED IN A MAZE

SONIA KRISHNA CHAND

MOTIVATION
CHAMPS
PUBLISHING

ISBN 978-1-956353-69-3
EBOOK 979-1-956353-70-9

(Sonia Krishna Chand / Motivation Champs)

The book was printed in the United States of America.

Special discount may apply on bulk quantities.
Please contact Motivation Champs Publishing to order.
www.motivationchamps.com

Cover Photo Compliments of Lakefront Pictures

DEDICATION

To my parents, who are a major reason why I am who I am today. To my brother Jay and my cousin Gargi—you played a major role in my life and supported my dream of writing this book when I started writing it back in 2005. To Autism Speaks Team Up, thank you for introducing me to a whole new world that would help me grow and become a person I love. To all the wonderful friends I have made throughout the years—thank you for all your love and support.

CONTENTS

FOREWORD

In the time I've spent getting to know Sonia Chand, I've come to recognize her as a storyteller who goes beyond recounting experiences; she offers a lifeline to those who have felt isolated, misunderstood, or marginalized. *Dropped in a Maze* is the culmination of her journey—an unapologetically honest account that sheds light on the struggles and triumphs of a life lived in defiance of conformity.

This book is for anyone who has ever felt out of place, as though they were navigating a world that wasn't designed with them in mind. Sonia's story doesn't merely detail her experiences; it dismantles the limitations imposed upon so many by cultural expectations, familial pressures, and societal norms. For those who, like Sonia, may be part of a community with deeply rooted traditions, this memoir reveals a path toward liberation, toward building a life that feels true to oneself. Sonia's words will resonate with readers on a deeply personal level, illuminating not only the journey of self-discovery but also the power that comes from fully embracing one's identity.

Throughout this book, Sonia explores the complexity of living with neurodiversity—a reality that affects countless individuals but is often misunderstood. Her narrative gives voice to those who live with conditions that make them uniquely gifted and yet, at times, marginalized. In a society that has not always celebrated difference, *"Dropped in a Maze"* serves as a resource and a roadmap, helping readers—especially leaders and professionals—understand how neurodiverse individuals enrich our world. Rather than viewing neurodivergent people as outliers, Sonia's story encourages us to recognize their strengths, their resilience, and their invaluable perspectives. This book, I believe, will inspire both individuals and businesses to see neurodiversity not as a challenge to be tolerated but as a strength to be embraced and integrated into all aspects of our lives and work.

Sonia's journey is not a straight path. Her memoir is aptly titled; life can feel like a maze, with twists, turns, and unexpected obstacles. But what makes Sonia's story truly extraordinary is her refusal to give up, even when the way forward seemed unclear. Her resilience offers hope to those who may be feeling overwhelmed or lost in their own labyrinths, reminding them that there is strength to be found in every misstep and every setback. Her journey is proof that even in the face of adversity, it is possible to rise, to claim your voice, and to live in a way that honors your truth.

One of the most striking aspects of Sonia's story is her courage to confront deeply ingrained cultural beliefs—especially within the South Asian community, where expectations about identity, mental health, and success can be both rigid and unspoken. For readers who share this heritage, Sonia's journey will resonate as a validation of their own experiences, offering them a sense of connection and the courage to question norms that may feel stifling. For readers from other backgrounds, her story will offer a window into the unique challenges faced by individuals who feel they must choose between their culture and their autonomy. In writing this book, Sonia has not only freed herself but has also given others permission to step out of the shadows and live more openly.

This memoir is as much a celebration of authenticity as it is an invitation to those who have felt compelled to hide parts of themselves in order to belong. Sonia writes about mental health, neurodiversity, and self-expression in a way that challenges readers to reframe what it means to be 'different.' Her story is not just her own; it is the story of countless individuals who have felt sidelined by a society that often values conformity over individuality. Sonia has lived these experiences and now shares them with a vulnerability that is both disarming and deeply inspiring. She shows us that the very qualities that make us feel different are often the same qualities that, when fully embraced, reveal our unique gifts.

As you read *Dropped in a Maze*, you may feel as though Sonia is speaking directly to you. Her words carry a rare authenticity that makes this book feel less like a memoir and more like a conversation with someone who understands what it means to struggle, to question, and to rise. Sonia does not claim to have all the answers; rather, she offers readers the tools to navigate their own journeys, to ask their own questions, and to find their own truths. For those who have ever felt that they don't quite fit the mold, this book serves as a reminder that there is beauty in difference, strength in vulnerability, and power in self-acceptance.

For businesses and organizations, *Dropped in a Maze* also stands as a powerful guide to understanding and valuing neurodiverse individuals. Sonia's insights offer practical lessons on how to create inclusive environments where everyone's unique talents are recognized and valued. In a world that is slowly beginning to understand the importance of diversity, Sonia's book pushes us to take this understanding a step further, to embrace neurodiversity not just as a concept but as a key component of a healthy and innovative society. Her story challenges us to think differently about what it means to succeed, to contribute, and to lead.

Sonia is a role model, a trailblazer, and an advocate for those who feel they have been dropped into a maze with no way out. But as she shows us in these pages, there is always a way forward. Her life, her words, and her spirit offer a beacon of hope for those who may be feeling lost. This book is a reminder that even in the most challenging moments, we have the power to reshape our paths, to define success on our own terms, and to create lives that are rich, meaningful, and true.

So, to every reader who feels misunderstood or out of place, let *Dropped in a Maze* be your guide. Let Sonia's story inspire you to find your own way, to embrace the parts of yourself that make you unique, and to step boldly into a world that needs your voice, your perspective, and your strength.

Vasavi Kumar: Author, Coach, LMSW

OPENING CAVEAT:
She's Different From Us

Monday, October 30, 1989, I went to school dressed in my usual school uniform. However, the day before, my family and I celebrated the Hindu New Year called Diwali. My parents thought it would be a great idea for me to take a box of chocolates to pass around to the class and for me to give them a short presentation about Diwali. Typically, Indian sweets are exchanged during Diwali. Instead of kids being excited to get a piece of chocolate, I heard a resounding "no thanks" when I walked around the class with the box. One classmate, Daveda, said loud and clear, "She's different from us."

I grew up not being diagnosed with autism spectrum disorder, formerly known as Asperger's Syndrome until I reached age 20. Being called names like 'weird' and 'different' and being made to feel like I don't 'live up' are not anomalies to me. A lot of times, people can be quick to judge and call someone 'weird' when they don't have an understanding about why a person is the way they are. Particularly, we think of the period of the '80s and '90s when I was growing up, how mental health was perceived. It had a much different vibe and was less openly discussed than it is today. The mentality of 'it's all in your head' very much rang true back then. However, for me, 'it's all in your head' takes on a different meaning because the autism spectrum is neurological. The brain is wired differently.

To say that the road was dark and lonely would not even begin to encapsulate the intensity of my feelings. What is it like to be on the autism spectrum? It is very much like being dropped in a maze trying to figure your way through to reach the other side. However, unlike others who are placed in the maze, you are blindfolded trying to navigate through. Other people, who are fully capable of seeing, can pick up on visual cues from others or look at the path that lies ahead of them to help them gain clues as to what direction to follow. A person who is blindfolded won't have such an opportunity, so they are left behind while everyone else is progressing.

There may be some individuals who are kind and patient enough to help the blindfolded person move through some of the maze, but they, too, want to get out of the maze and may become frustrated and leave the person behind. Other people may just resort to teasing and bullying because they don't understand why a person on the autism spectrum struggles with things that come more intuitively to other individuals.

Despite facing challenges with being on the autism spectrum, I was still able to accomplish great things in my life. Case in point, I went to law school, got an LL.M in Financial Services, passed the New York Bar exam, and worked on Wall Street. In my search to discover my true self, I came to learn that law was not my calling. In fact, I always knew it wasn't the right career for me deep inside, but I was always too timid to be vociferous about it to my parents.

I eventually found my calling and went on to attain a master's in Clinical Mental Health. Today, I am working as a psychotherapist and, more importantly, help clients on the autism spectrum. I also run marathons to raise awareness for Autism Speaks Team Up.

I was aired on NBC to speak about why I run for Autism Speaks Team Up. The book you are about to read illustrates some of the social and emotional challenges people, especially women with autism spectrum disorder, go through from an insider's perspective. While I tell my story openly and honestly, I do not intend for this book to blame individuals. To protect individuals and entities at large, I have changed the names of individuals, towns, and schools. Characters in the memoir are not designed to play a guessing game of 'Who's Who' but rather to give context to the world as I interpreted and received it.

Throughout the book, you will hear me speak about my family, as they obviously played an important role in life. I had an elder brother, Jay, who was five years older than me. He unfortunately passed away from cancer in 2009 at only 31 years old.

I am writing this book so that people understand how the autism spectrum manifests and how a person may see the world. This book is to help people on the autism spectrum feel seen, heard, and supported. Also, let's not forget parents of children on the autism spectrum, spouses of those on the autism spectrum, and children of parents on the autism spectrum. This is all for you.

Chapter 1

WELCOME TO THE MAZE

I attended kindergarten in an elite private K-12 school called Lake Point Academy (LPA). Most of kindergarten is vague. Two incidents stand out as moments in my life as ways that people saw me differently. I started to also feel disconnected and in my own world.

JANUARY 11, 1988

The images were vivid of me sitting with the class on the rug with a huge calendar up front. The teacher would go over how to tell the date. 1988 was the year. Every day at school was practice for us to recite calendar dates. I grew bored of having to learn the dates every day, mostly because I didn't understand how they would apply in life. Therefore, I missed the fact that from a social and even legal standpoint, dates would be needed, especially upon signing important documents.

My focus would drift, and I would daydream instead of the trip my family took to India to attend a cousin's wedding, but more so, I would daydream about the Air France 747-100 Combi we flew in. I was fascinated by the plane's design at large. I was taken in by the movement. Moreover, I was fascinated by the vents on the ceiling, and I spent a good portion of time looking at those vents during the whole flight. I remember briefly watching a countdown to a movie starting on the projection screen, but I fixated on one thing alone: the airplane vents. It is a very common trait of people with autism to fixate on a certain thing, but what people fixate on varies. I was more fascinated by the aircraft than I was by the trip at large. In fact, my mind would daydream about that aircraft for a good portion of my young childhood.

Despite being somewhat bored with the repetition of learning about dates, I didn't like change very well. In fact, the teacher told my mom in a meeting that I would get very upset when the garbage can was moved. I would pick the garbage can and place it back to where I was used to seeing it. It was a peculiarity, amongst others, that rang out to the teacher as clear as a bell.

Another peculiarity was recess time. Teachers told my mother that I would not interact or play with other kids, but rather I would be on the swingset and not want to get off until recess was over.

The last memory I have of LPA was the show-and-tell. Whereas other kids picked up on the idea that you show and tell something, such as your favorite toy or talk about your favorite story, my show and tell involved something unique and impromptu. I was afraid of breaking the rules because the teacher told us to be creative and not just copy someone else. Unlike other students, I took her words very literally and did not bring in a favorite toy like the rest of them. Lo and behold, this is a symptom of being on the autism spectrum: taking things very literally.

I was completely unprepared for show-and-tell, but I did my best to make up something on the spot. I spoke about how kids were able to make shapes with their hands and illustrated how if you pressed your index fingers and thumbs together, you could make a diamond. The teacher put on a good act of seeming impressed.

It was decided shortly after that I go to another school for the next academic year, which would've been my first-grade year. The school and my parents collaboratively felt I wasn't fit for Lake Point Academy.

Instead, my parents decided to enroll me in a school closer to the house, which was a k-8 parochial school. What's paradoxical about that decision is we weren't even Catholic, but my parents had attended parochial schools before. They were left with a good impression about the quality of education they received, and they wanted that for me. All of this was just the beginning of navigating the twists and turns of the maze.

Chapter 2

STRUGGLING TO BELONG

UNDERSTANDING SCHOOL AND INTRODUCTIONS TO ENSUING PUNISHMENT

St. Margaret's Academy was the first real awakening I received to what school was really about. I was completely confused and overwhelmed dealing with a classroom, students, and sensory issues. The class was organized into four rows of desks. I was shocked at how people helped me when I dropped a box of crayons on the floor, and the students around me helped me pick up the crayons. I didn't expect that this was a social behavior, a common courtesy to be mindful of others and help others. This was the start of the maze. The class was predominantly White. There were perhaps two other Blacks and one Filipino girl. I was the only Indian Hindu in my class. The cultural and religious background wasn't remarkable apart from when the class had to attend church services, and I sat and observed everyone break hosts with the priest.

I also was different from other students in the way my brain gathered information. I wasn't as quick to gather information, and it was hard to adjust to everything all at once. I know that it is easier to grasp information when given a system on how to do things. An example would be if the teacher had a step-by-step process on how to get organized by illustrating that we put homework papers in folders. We also have different folders for different subjects. Clearly, mapping things out is what came in handy for me to best learn.

Apart from adjusting to trying to learn by what the teacher's style was, I also had to learn to deal with classmates and sensory sounds. I remember the first time ever hearing a fire alarm go off. Even though it was loud for everyone, that was the biggest sensory assault to my ears. My hearing was hypersensitive which meant that loud sounds only intensified.

First grade in and of itself was just confounding. The only things that stood out were my spelling book cover, which made the balloons look 3-D, and Mrs. Drescher's demeanor. She didn't have a lot of patience and was short-tempered. In all fairness, in first grade, we already knew that I was coming in with some social and learning problems, but because of the lack of knowledge available about females on the autism spectrum, no diagnosis of autism was given at that time.

Teachers weren't familiar with disabilities nor as compassionate to students who were neurodivergent as many teachers are now. The end of the year sparked a notable moment for me. The class was assigned to bring a baby picture for show and tell. For some reason, most probably because I forgot about it, I didn't bring my baby picture. The punishment was quite harsh in that the teacher didn't allow me to sit with the rest of the class in the show-and-tell activity.

This shows the danger of ignorance and being too quick to punish. What could've been done instead was perhaps to have it written on a piece of paper and put in a folder to bring in the baby picture. Another thing the teacher could've done was ensure that the folder was placed in the backpack so when it was checked at night, the assignment was sure to be in the backpack the next morning.

KEY TAKEAWAY: Early intervention to learn how a child on the autism spectrum learns and helps them develop a system is so important to help them get set up for success. It is unfortunate that most of the time, we tend to punish those we don't understand. Please remember, it's not always because a person being punished is horrible and deserving of such. It's that people actually need help, and they may not have the skills to say, "I need some help." After all, what can you expect out of a 6-year-old who doesn't quite understand her own mind yet?

PROBLEM CHILD: NO, NOT THE MOVIE

'Learning and social problems' became more pronounced when second grade started. The second-grade teacher, Mrs. Schmidt, appeared to be in her early 60s at best. She was a rigid teacher with no tolerance for anything outside the straight and narrow. She held students to rigorous standards, akin to those you see students held to in *Dead Poet's Society*. My organization skills and learning were still poor coming into second grade.

One day in class, she unexpectedly asked us to pull out a worksheet that she had given us a few days before. I tried to look for it, but my desk was a bit discombobulated. She noticed that I didn't have my worksheet, and she came over and looked at the inside of my desk. She then took the desk and physically dumped it out, with all the contents falling to the floor. I felt ashamed of myself and embarrassed. Out of shame and embarrassment, I looked around the room. I saw people looking flabbergasted. I was made to get down on the floor on my knees and clean up in front of the whole class to bear witness to. Mrs. Schmidt dumped my desk out at least three consecutive times thereafter that same day until the desk looked 'good enough.'

This once again stresses the importance of a system and not being so quick to be ignorant on behalf of people who work with those on the autism spectrum. Some kids need to be taught about folders and how to properly place material in folders. Some kids need to be taught how to organize the inside of a desk. If a kid has a discombobulated desk, it's not because the kid is purposefully acting insubordinate. Often, the kid may need that extra help.

While I was on the floor picking materials up, I went into daydream mode to prevent myself from crying and making a bigger scene in front of the class. I imagined I was getting advice from my dad. "You know, Sonu, the same things happened to me when I was your age. Teachers were rude to me, too, and I was bullied like you. However, I became a success story, and I know you can too."

My reputation of being seen as 'the problem' started to solidify amongst the students. Like at every school, there is always the 'teacher's pet.' This time, it was a group of girls in the bathroom. They tried hard to emulate Mrs. Schmidt, and in retrospect, those girls probably deserved drama club awards for 1. their efforts which really were more of them trying too hard, and 2. an award for being the biggest kiss butts. The school might as well have given them sparkling grape juice in champagne flutes, too.

The girls (even though I could really use a word that means female dogs, but I don't want to insult the animals) gave me a lecture about how I was a bad student who couldn't keep up with the class. They were haranguing me to no end about how I would be a failure. One of the girls, Peggy, tried to be 'nice' towards the end of the harangue by saying, "Sorry to break your heart, Sonia."

All the other girls turned a blind eye while I just stood there and cried. I went back to the classroom in tears, and Mrs. Schmidt surprisingly told off Peggy, alongside her other friends Julia and Daveda.

One morning in class, Mrs. Schmidt announced a rule that if a person has a birthday party and invites one person, the whole class has to be invited. I thought that because it was a rule, students would follow through with it. People on the autism spectrum tend to take things very literally and are rule-oriented, therefore understanding that a rule is something that has to be followed and will be followed by everyone. Truth is, not everyone follows the rules.

I learned that Julia was having a birthday party, and she announced that she would be send out invitations to the class. The day came when she handed out invitations.

I still hadn't received an invite by the time recess came around, so I went to ask Julia about it. I hoped I could win friends over by being invited to the party. I was desperate to prove to others that I was a cool person to be around and that I was not the problem child that Mrs. Schmidt convincingly made me out to be. I was just a kid who struggled and needed proper professional help in hindsight. Julia told me that there were too many people, and her mother made her cut one person. Therefore, she couldn't invite me. The whole "I had to cut one person" kind of excuse would not be the last time I would hear something like this. This really was code for "I didn't want to invite you," but just a 'nicer' way of saying it.

I wanted to make sure I wasn't the only one who was excluded from being invited to the birthday party. I went around the room, asking people if they were invited, and they all answered "yes."

However, when I made my way around to Daveda, she was quite taken aback that I approached her while she was talking to her friends.

"Excuse me, but you're not in this conversation," Daveda remarked snarkily.

"I was just wanting to ask if you were invited to…"

"Yes, I was invited. Are you done now?" Daveda cut me off before I could even complete the question.

I went back to my desk feeling quite depressed. I felt humiliated that I was singled out, and I was in a lot of pain from the constant lambasting in front of the class by the teacher, let alone the students. In retrospect, if a teacher is always lambasting a student for being 'no good,' how were other students supposed to respect that student? This goes to show how powerful a teacher can be and how a teacher can set an example of behavior for students to follow.

KEY TAKEAWAY: Teachers have incredible influence and hold an immense amount of power. It's so important to have a strong rapport between parents and teachers. A lot of issues that start emerging could be worked on early together as a team. Rote learning about having a system in place for a kid on the autism spectrum is so helpful and beneficial to help ensure that kid's success.

Kids learn what they see. They are impressionable at a young age. Teach them to be kind while they are young. Teach them that not all kids who are constantly in trouble are defiant or bad kids.

YOU STICK OUT A LITTLE

My desperation to try to make friends started to slowly simmer throughout elementary school. I began to channel some of this desperation by throwing birthday parties. I was determined to show classmates I was smart, and I was determined to show people that they were wrong about me all along. In retrospect, people really didn't want me around throughout the year. The birthday parties consisted of people whom I thought I could have a chance at winning as they weren't popular girls but people in the middle of the hierarchy. In retrospect, a lot of the people I invited were driven more out of shame that I didn't have anybody I could genuinely say was a real friend. Some people who were invited didn't deserve to be invited, for instance, Anabela and Jessica. Anabela actively bullied me with a fellow classmate, Blossom, towards the end of fourth grade.

There was a reason Blossom got angry with me, and that was because I wrote a mean note about her friend Rachel. Throughout fourth grade in general, Blossom along with her best friends Rachel and Phoebe, used to laugh at me. I never understood why. Perhaps there were cues I was emitting, but I was socially blinded to them.

This is very common with people on the autism spectrum as they don't always understand how they come across to others. They may be doing peculiar behaviors that they may not realize they are doing, but others will sure be quick to pick up on them. Such behaviors include stimming behaviors. My stimming behavior of choice was rocking and leg jitters.

Another way that a person on the autism spectrum can stand out is by not 'fitting in' to community standards. Forest Ridge was very much the type of town where people followed the unwritten rule: You had to keep up with the Joneses. People as young as my grade were very cautious about what outfits they wore, making sure they went shopping periodically so as to not wear the same outfits redundantly, had a sense of accessories and changing things up in terms of outfit and accessory selection, and had impeccable hygiene.

I was not fashion savvy and thoughts of shopping never crossed my mind. People were not afraid to comment on my clothes or earrings. "Is that the only pair of earrings you have? You keep wearing the same clothes over and over again, and you never go shopping for new clothes." I also was not showering regularly or putting on deodorant. In fact, I didn't know what deodorant was until Jessica brought it up to me one day.

"Can I ask you a personal question?" asked Jessica.

"Yeah," I replied.

"Do you wear deodorant?"

"No."

"Maybe you need to look into buying yourself a deodorant stick. This is perhaps why people say you smell bad."

I used to cry too much in fourth grade due to the hypersensitivity of people making fun of me and not liking me. This was another way I was alienating myself. This once again goes to the system that on top of people on the autism spectrum needing to have a system to organize and process information, they also need to be taught social skills. Things that come intuitively for neurotypicals (a term used to describe people who are not on the autism spectrum) need to be taught to those on the autism spectrum.

This is where social skills training comes in very handy and even essential. Good social skills training would include how to:

- Make and keep friends.

- Conversation skills.

- Read social cues and understand non-verbal communication.

- Know when to give up on trying to befriend someone.

- Handle social situations with regards to conflict, differentiating playful teasing versus bullying, and how to respond to snarky comments from peers appropriately.

- Regulate emotions in healthy and peer-appropriate ways so that one is not considered to be a 'cry baby,' for instance:

(More about social skills and the dangers of failing to intervene will be discussed in Chapter 3.)

People eventually got tired of my cries. Teachers would intervene at times and try to figure out what was the matter. It was from there that Rachel started getting the impression I was being a tattle-tale. Rachel made threatening jab cross punching motions to me during class. Blossom told me at recess one day that Rachel was going to hurt me and to be careful. In retaliation, I wrote a nasty note about Rachel meant for my eyes, but it somehow accidentally dropped on the floor in the coat section of the room. The note basically said, *"At my next birthday party, I will ask Blossom to bring her Ouija board so that I can ask when Rachel will die because that is how much I hate her."*

Of course, Rachel was hurt and upset. I didn't think she was the type of person who would get hurt feelings, especially from someone like me. In my mind, I thought she did such a good job bullying others; how can she get hurt feelings? It is common for many people on the autism spectrum to not understand where someone else is coming from. In retrospect, the reason why Rachel used to bully was because, in fact, she herself was a hurt and insecure person. There is a reason for the saying 'hurt people hurt people.'

The person who was the most angry about the note was Blossom. She had a right to be because what I did wasn't okay. Two wrongs don't make a right, ever. Despite the teacher getting involved in the situation about the note, the teacher placed me to sit next to Blossom and Anabela towards the end of the semester.

I don't think the teacher was quite aware of Blossom's ensuing wrath. The desks were shaped with square designs, but because of the odd number of students, there was one seating arrangement that was shaped in triangular form. I sat at the tip of the triangle. The teasing and taunting between Blossom and Anabela were relentless.

"Anabela, Sonia smells really bad," said Blossom.

"I know. She is so annoying," replied Anabela.

"I bet she doesn't even know that Jessica doesn't want to be her friend anymore," said Blossom.

"I think maybe we should tell Sonia, that way poor Jessica doesn't keep getting annoyed by Sonia," said Anabela.

Jessica was someone whom I considered to be a best friend at one point, alongside Tina and Mary. All the girls were in different homerooms when I first met them: Tina and Mary were part of the gifted class and remained that way throughout elementary school. I thought things were starting to turn around at one point in the friendship trajectory, but the girls all eventually quit being friends with me.

Understandably, they grew tired of my hypersensitivity, crying, and lack of peer-appropriate social skills to make and maintain friendships.

Sure enough, Blossom and Jacob tried to get Jessica to confess to really not liking me all along.

"Jessica, come here," Blossom ordered as she stood next to me and Jacob.

"What's going on?" asked Jessica in a bewildered tone of voice.

"I think you should tell Sonia how you really feel about her. You have been telling practically everyone in the whole grade that you really didn't like Sonia and were only pretending to like her," said Blossom.

"What are you talking about?" asked Jessica.

"I don't think it's fair to either yourself or Sonia to keep a secret like this about her for one whole year," said Jacob.

Jessica didn't even bother to continue the conversation, but rather, she walked off in a rather cowardly manner.

This left me feeling beside myself, and I wondered why Jessica didn't firmly stick up for the friendship I thought we had. After all, Blossom stood up for Rachel, and that was what I thought was an example of a true friend.

Jessica told me she was mad at me for how I behaved earlier that year when I pranked Jacob's home. Yes, I pranked Jacob's home as a way to retaliate against all the bullying. Unfortunately, Blossom got blamed for pranking Jacob's home. However, she was the one who ended up telling on me to Jacob and the rest of the class for what I had done. It wasn't fair to Blossom, and I owned up to behaving poorly. In retrospect, I didn't have the social skills to self-advocate in a way that would be considered socially appropriate to peers my age.

After the short conversation I had with Jessica after the recess encounter with Blossom and Jacob, I asked her if she was still mad about the prank I had done earlier. She told me she was not, but she also told me not to tell Blossom about it.

I left the conversation still feeling bewildered, maybe even more so. Why wouldn't Jessica want Blossom to know? I took Jessica's words at face value because of my ability, especially back then, to take people's words at face value. As I reflect, I think a part of me was scared about even the thought of being friendless, even though that was the reality. I was afraid of the shame that I felt, and the shame acted very much like the monster you wanted to run away from. Unfortunately, when you are trapped in a maze, it's even more of a burden to figure out what path to run down to escape the monster.

In retrospect, the reason Jessica didn't want Blossom to know that she wasn't mad at me anymore was because Jessica herself wasn't a real friend. Jessica was living the fake lie that everyone was calling her out on. And, if she wasn't honest with me, she, in fact, wasn't even being honest or loyal to Blossom, even though those two ended up supposedly becoming 'friends' as elementary school went on.

My lack of social skills and inability to make and keep friends led me to try to win over friends by throwing birthday parties for the same classmates who weren't loyal or real. The people who would attend the birthday parties just treated our house like it was some kind of museum.

The perfect example happened at the birthday party I threw in our last year of elementary school. A group of girls got on the treadmill and ran on it as if it were some kind of toy. The treadmill belt broke, and my mom had to get it repaired.

People were also using the phone and pranking people. People did not respond well to the prank calls. There was one lady who called back and threatened to call the police. As I reflect back, I started to think to myself about how these people would've never behaved like that in their own homes, let alone the homes of their other peers. I remember my mom and brother saying something similar about people's behaviors when they came to my house: They thought the people were just using me to play and run around a big house. Case in point, people didn't act like this at Jessica's birthday parties, at least the ones I got invited to before I was not invited anymore.

The people who attended the birthday party weren't people worthy of extending an invitation to. At the end, the only person I was truly tricking was myself because if people liked me or accepted me for the person I was already, chances were highly unlikely that a birthday party would change anything. If anything, it gave people another way to manipulate or take advantage of me.

The party eventually settled down, and people played some games. This only happened after I ended up having a breakdown and in tears. I got too overwhelmed. I sensed the disappointment with how people acted and how it affected my parents' moods. My mom intervened to help me regroup and calm down. She didn't really have to do much except ask me what was wrong, audible enough for other people to get the hint to cut the act.

People spent the night, as it was a slumber party. They were having conversations about whom they were crushing on. Truth is, I started to develop a crush on Jacob. People went around in a circle, sharing who they were crushing on. Before I knew it, it was my turn. It was then that I told people that I had a crush on Jacob, but I begged everybody not to tell Jacob. Even though everyone said collectively that night that they would keep the secret confined within themselves, do you really think they were telling the truth?

Sure enough, when Monday morning rolled around, Blossom called me to the corner.

"Hey Sonia, can you come here for a minute?" she asked.

"Yes?"

"Sonia, I know who you like."

"What do you mean? I asked in a rather shocking way. I thought those girls would uphold their word, but in all honesty, those girls weren't even true and loyal from the get-go."

"All your friends told me," said Blossom.

"Told you what?"

"They told me whom you liked."

"I don't like anybody."

"Yes, you do! Your friends all came to me and told me what they heard from you at your birthday party."

"Okay, fine. I like Jacob Stern. Please don't say anything to him or anyone else."

"Oh no, totally," she said.

Seriously folks, do you really think she kept her word? Recess ended, and I was standing in line to go inside the school.

"Sonia, you like me?! Ewww! I would never go out with someone like you!" This was followed by an uproar of laughter.

One of the bedrocks of having autism spectrum is the intense interests that occupy the mind. While everyone differs in what their intense interests are, mine always were about people, particularly when I developed intense crushes on men. Friendships were another intense interest for me, partly due to the high level of difficulty it was for me and still somewhat is today. Other interests spanned into accomplishing achievements and certain material things. I used to spend a lot of time fantasizing about what it would be like to be Jacob's girlfriend.

Back in third grade, the swing sets became my place of refuge. Now, here I was again, using the swing sets as a place to process and think about Jacob and all the bullying and backstabbing from the girls. I enjoyed the back-and-forth sensation of the swing and the fact that I felt like I was flying each time I swung. The swings were where I allowed myself to slip into my own imaginary world: a world where I was finally a favorite and accepted by teachers and peers. I used to imagine being a famous person who had fans and media coverage. It's easy to glorify fame that much more when you are a person who isn't accepted. You imagine how great it could feel to finally have people giving you attention and acceptance, notwithstanding all the things that get taken away when a person becomes famous.

The swing sets were where I used to imagine what it would be like to be Jacob's girlfriend. I imagined what it was like getting to know his family. I heard he had two sisters who were extremely popular and pretty. I used to write letters in my diary that would be addressed to Jacob, where I was looking for the answer of, "Why don't you like me?" Deep down, I was looking for validation that something was inherently wrong with me. I always felt abnormal. I just needed someone to tell me that and tell me how to become normal. Even though I wasn't directly getting answers from Jacob as to what was wrong with me, I was eventually able to get feedback from someone else.

THE NASTY TRUTH

During the course of the year, we ended up getting a few new students who moved to Forest Ridge. One happened to be Patricia, a blast from the past, from Forest Green. Patrcia and I were classmates at the public school in Forest Green when I made my Indian parents proud by failing second grade at St. Margaret's Academy. Woo hoo!!!

This time around, Patricia and I became friends. Patricia made friends with others in the class, and she was able to get along with everyone relatively well. I started getting feedback from Patricia about what classmates thought or said about me. Some of the feedback was a repeat from the previous year. Patricia told me that people like Blossom, Rachel, and Phoebe used to make fun of the fact that I wasn't fashion-savvy. Patricia also mentioned the rumor that Jessica only 'pretends' to be my friend.

More conversations and events seemed to unfold as the semester carried through. I had a candid conversation with Patricia.

"Patricia, why can't I ever seem to fit in? All the other Indian kids at this school seem to fit in."

"Sonia, it is because you stick out a little. You cry a lot. You need to learn to shake things off."

"I try too."

"You need to try a bit harder. You cry much more than what is normal. You need to learn to not take things so seriously." This wasn't the first time I was told this, and it wouldn't be the last for that year.

Patricia had other candid conversations with me as the semester progressed. She used to teach me comebacks to say to people. So, the next time someone calls you stupid, you just ask them, "Did your mom drop you on your head as a baby?"

There was a time when we had to do a how-to-speech. I chose to illustrate how to make a bracelet using beads and putting it on a thread. I didn't have the skills to choose something else. For the class presentation, I tried to put the bead on the thread. For some reason, I just wasn't able to fit the bead on. I don't know if it was my anxiety, but Patricia had to come and help me. Afterward, Patricia wasn't as kind.

"Sonia, you need to start figuring out stuff for yourself. Everyone thinks you are such a baby!"

"Who?" I asked.

"Practically, everyone. You never can do anything yourself. Everyone has to do everything for you, such as the day you did the bead presentation. I had to help you when you should've done that on your own!"

It was hard to hear, and I can understand now why classmates thought I was a baby. People saw how I struggled and needed extra support academically in ways that others didn't need. The inappropriate amount of times I cried at school was another giveaway that could easily lead people to think of me as less than a baby.

THE TRUTH COMES OUT TO MOM

My family came to learn the truth towards the end of fifth grade. The class took a field trip to a famous camping ground in southern Indiana. The whole point of the field trip was for us to learn about how the early settlers lived. The class spent the night at the camp. We were assigned cabins with chaperones to each.

During the day, we did activities such as sitting in an old schoolhouse and learning a lesson. We also made and ate Johnny Cakes. At night, we were assigned to perform skits around the campfire. The skits ended with the principal and two other teachers doing their own skit together and allowing for a question and answer from students. It was very comical, and people asked all sorts of funny questions. After the campfire skits were done, the principal offered students the option to go for a walk on the campground trail.

A lot of people were walking with their friend groups, and I was alone.

My frustrations had built up, and my thoughts started racing during the walk. I was bewildered as to why I kept having lingering difficulties socially. I was saddened that the other efforts I put in that year, such as performing a jazz dance in the talent show and doing a Bollywood dance for the school as part of a social studies project, all ended up in not achieving the end goal. I started screaming out loud, "I hate myself!"

Jacob was walking with his friends, and he asked me, "Hey Sonia, do you want to kill yourself?"

Without thinking it through, I said, "Yeah."

Jacob just turned around and said, "Okay."

The next thing I knew, I shouted, "I want to kill myself because that is how much I hate myself!"

People didn't respond well to that.

"Sonia, can you just stop it?!" exclaimed Misty, a classmate. Nobody else said anything after, and they just continued on with conversing with their friend groups.

I remained quiet for the remainder of the walk. I looked up at the night sky. There was a full moon surrounded by stars everywhere. It was a picturesque night sky, one that represented calmness and beauty. It was a sky that represented where stories ran deep. I thought to myself, "It would be nice to be there and be part of the beauty." I was looking for the calm in the never-ending storm.

The serenity ended abruptly once the field trip ended and we were back at school. I was met with constant badgering mainly from Misty and some others, about what I said at camp. "Did you mean what you said? Why do you want to kill yourself? Are you sure you're not suicidal? Why do you want to kill yourself? Do you have a plan? Were you serious?" It didn't take long for the teacher to find out what I said. She had a meeting with my mom after school, and I was introduced to a psychiatrist shortly after that.

In summary, having a system where someone understands social skills and how to handle situations are paramount when a person on the autism spectrum is young. One thing parents may want to consider is spending at least an hour a day on social skills training or sending a child to a professional who teaches social skills.

Pay attention to what is happening outside of school. How often is your kid invited to someone's house or to birthday parties? How often do you see your kid socializing with others in real-time? The quicker a person can get access to help, the better the outcomes can start to be so that a mention of suicide is nowhere on the radar.

Also, no matter how bad your life feels and how lonely and empty you feel, the world is better with you IN IT than without. You are here for a reason. There are people who look up to you and may need you more than you realize. All the rejections, bullying, and ostracism that you go through with peers will one day turn into a gift, even though it is very hard to see in the moment.

Chapter 3

THE BREAKDOWN

FIRST ATTEMPTS AT THERAPY AND TECHNICALLY COOL LESSONS FROM MISTY

Upon first meeting, Dr. Kim seemed very irritable. She did not ask questions in a friendly manner and seemed condescending. She did, however, prescribe Ritalin. That medication was not new for me. I had been on other ADHD medication for my repeat of second grade, but I don't remember having to take medication in the third or fourth grades. Dr. Kim also assigned me to her social worker, Antoinette, for the talk therapy portion. Individual psychotherapy was a new concept for me completely, and I didn't know what to expect. One thing I found quite annoying about Antoinette was the way she kept asking questions back at me instead of understanding that I struggled with peers.

"People in my grade told me I don't dress well, am smelly, and act babyish," I explained.

"What about your clothes? Why are people saying this to you?" Antoinette questioned.

"I don't know. I was told by my tutor, Mrs. Goldestein (the same homeroom teacher I had for fourth grade who became my tutor for 5th-8th grade), I am an easy target."

"What makes you an easy target?"

"I don't know. Perhaps the feedback I got."

"What about the feedback you got?"

"What I told you people said."

I didn't have the intellect quite yet to be introspective, as I found the world and myself rather confounding. I was being treated as an adult rather than the 11-year-old child that I was. There needed to be more rapport-building between the therapist and me. I felt she could've done some ice-breakers and even some therapeutic games as a way to start. Once that was established, I needed a more hands-on kind of therapy. This would entail hands-on training where social cues, how to interact with others, what girls talk about at middle school age, how to handle conflicts, and how to stand up for myself when the going got tough were taught.

Ritalin was not going to teach me those things, but instead, it helped me lose a bit of weight due to loss of appetite. I remember mentioning my concerns to one of the special education teachers, and she told me, "You have to force yourself to eat, Sonia. Otherwise you could get very sick."

I used to leave therapy sessions feeling frustrated because it always seemed like the same dialogue each week.

"So, why do you think kids don't like you? What about your clothes?"

I never felt we were getting anything accomplished; I felt like a hamster on the wheel. I told my mom I didn't want to go see Antoinette anymore after a couple sessions. She didn't oppose me on that.

While I was quitting therapy, Misty and a group of other girls from class had a 'meeting' with each other. Misty happened to be a newcomer to Forest Ridge, but she had the social skills to just fit right in as if she had been at our school all along. Misty became friends with many girls right away.

Misty and the other girls discussed my crying behaviors, hygiene, clothes, and swinging behaviors during recess. Misty was the speaker for everyone, expressing what she thought.

"I've decided that we are all going to help you become technically cool. Here are some things we need to tackle: 1. Your hygiene. You need to start being more regular about taking a shower. I hate to say this to you, but sometimes you kind of smell."

I replied, "I have been taking showers."

"You need to do them consistently and often."

Misty was correct in what she was saying. I needed to be mindful of how often I was taking a shower because I could go for days and forget about it. Also, I had issues with the temperature change from getting into a warm shower to getting out where it was cooler. Misty taught me to use the thermostat in the hallway and crank it up. Therefore, it was a system that worked! Hygiene is a huge part of the unwritten social skills piece because people don't really want to interact with someone who has poor hygiene or a pungent odor.

Misty had more to offer: "You need to work on going shopping and buying clothes." You need to learn to dress like others. Also, you need to stop swinging on the swing sets at recess. That is not considered cool for a fifth grader. And you need to stop crying so much."

"Why do I need to stop the swing sets? I love going on them!" I protested.

"Because it's not cool anymore! Swinging is for kids; we're about to be middle schoolers soon."

"What am I supposed to do during recess?" I inquired, quite exasperated.

"Anything else but swing."

"As for my clothes, what am I supposed to do?"

"You need to learn how to pick out your own outfits that are cool and hip."

"My mom does a lot of my shopping."

"You need to get her to stop buying you clothes. You need to pick your own clothes."

I had no clue about how to dress like my peers. I was always different in how I picked out clothes.

I tried to heed Misty's advice about not swinging on the swing sets by going to hang out with Misty and her friends. One of the girls saw me, and she asked me to leave because they were 'talking.' "Can you go and swing or something? We are talking. Thanks."

And just like that, I was off to the swing sets! It was paradoxical that, on the one hand, Misty was telling me that swing sets were not cool anymore. On the other hand, she stayed radio silent when I was suggested to go swing by her friend because the group was 'talking.' Sometimes, people are hard to understand.

KEY TAKEAWAY #1: If a therapist didn't work out the first time, it's important for parents to consider looking into other options instead of firing a therapist without a backup. Be intentional about what you want your child to get help for, and be vociferous when speaking to potential therapists.

KEY TAKEAWAY #2: It's important to be mindful of your hygiene. Remember to have a system where you shower every day or at least every other day. Remember to wear deodorant and perhaps put on some body spray, perfume, or cologne.

WELCOME TO SIXTH GRADE

I could not have been more excited for the first day of school! I was going to be in middle school, and I was going to have a huge, fresh start. I already had people I knew and liked from summer school. I had a cute new outfit from The Limited. It was an outfit I saw on a mannequin, and I knew I needed to copy the look. I was still nowhere close to understanding fashion. The outfit was red shorts, a red shirt that said *The Limited* inside a star on the shirt, and a white crochet vest over it. The outfit coincidentally matched my glasses that had red circular frames.

The middle school excitement wore off rather quickly within the first week, especially after witnessing the moody attitude of my math teacher, Mrs. Stephens. I guess she had an excuse to be moody: she was pregnant. Mrs. Stephens was set to take off towards the end of the Fall Semester for maternity leave. She made sure to make life pure hell every day during second period.

"Sonia, what are you doing? Can't you keep up with what we are doing?!" was often the sentiment at first. She was intimidating, and I was scared to even ask for help or clarification on what we were going over in class. My struggle to keep up with her class set me up to be made an example of. Things got so bad in Mrs. Stephens' math class that she gave me a 10-minute after-school detention in front of the whole class.

There were times I didn't even want to attend her class, and I ditched her class on occasion during the semester. I overheard Mrs. Stephens call the front office on their intercom system, and she asked if they saw me because I wasn't in class. I was at the guidance office, which was located right in the back of the front office.

I started going to my guidance counselor, Mrs. Horowitz, to try to get help and support. At first glance, she was very kind and compassionate. She spoke in a very soft manner. The first time I went there was to discuss my concerns about friendships. I was noticing how friend groups were starting to form and solidify. However, I felt like I was not fitting in nor connecting with others in quite the same way other classmates were. I was always outed or othered in the sense that people didn't respond to me in the same way they would others. People would either give short answers to my questions or ignore me.

I started to give Mrs. Horowitz my background history of elementary school hardships with friends. The goal was so she could understand where I was coming from. I wanted to make clear that friendship-making issues were not a new concept just because I entered middle school. She took the paper, wrote down things such as third grade, and threw it in the trash. In retrospect, I understand what she was trying to do. She thought if I could just forget about the issues I had in elementary school, it would be easier to focus on the present. However, it wasn't quite that simple. After all, if it was that simple to just forget about painful experiences and just throw things from the past behind us, mental health professionals would not be in business.

There was processing and healing that needed to be done from the past pain of elementary school. There was a system that needed to be set in place socially. While others were moving ahead in the maze, I fell further and further behind.

THE CHEER

Usually, we had different teachers for the different subjects, but for Reading and English, we had the same teacher. Between classes, people would either stay in the classroom or leave to hang out. I remember just feeling so lonely that I made up a cheer about Jacob out of nowhere. The cheer went: "Jacob Stern is the sexiest male alive!" People saw it and laughed. I was happy that I was finally getting some attention.

The next day, after lunch, I went to stand outside. I thought the whole thing was forgotten until Sheila, one of my classmates, approached me.

"Hey Sonia, do that cheer you did the other day."

"What cheer?"

"You know. The one that goes like this," and she showed me the arm movements. Then, I was able to remember it, and I was ready to perform.

Before I began, she said, "Hey, wait a minute. Let me go get some people," and off she went.

Her friends included people who were in the popular crew. Sure enough, they gathered around. I started cheering. People laughed and applauded. The next day, after lunch, I performed the cheer again. I had an even bigger crowd that time around. People laughed, and I performed more. I felt a dopamine rush to my head, and I never had that kind of elated feeling before. As much as I fed off the energy of people laughing to perform more cheers, I never quite understood why people were laughing.

In an attempt to get answers, I called up one girl who used to laugh with the crowd. She just told me that she laughed because other people were laughing. She didn't give a reason. I was still bewildered as to what was so funny about the cheer. Nevertheless, it made me feel good to get any kind of attention, not knowing that the attention given was negative.

Doing the cheer took up the whole lunch period, and I started doing it every day for the rest of that week. Kiera, one of the popular girls who was a fellow classmate, used to tell people to "stand back and enjoy the show."

It wasn't long before Jacob became aware of the cheers, and he stood with the crowd and watched me perform it. At first, he was shocked, and he was like, "Oh, my God." Jacob's face turned beet red out of embarrassment. I never intended to embarrass or hurt him in any way. I was only focused on how I could make friends.

While I was going on with these cheers, Rosie came outside and said, "Sonia, Jacob doesn't like you doing that. He just wants you to make a fool of yourself." I did not believe her. She said this in front of Jacob, and he stayed reticent.

Kiera had me do the cheers for the upperclassmen, but they didn't laugh. I even heard someone ask, "Your point is?"

One of the upperclassmen who saw the cheer was a classmate from gym class. After class, she came up to me and asked, "Do you like embarrassing yourself?"

"No, I don't like embarrassing myself."

"So, why are you doing those cheers?" she asked in disbelief.

In my mind, I didn't even fathom that I was embarrassing myself. If anything, I was excited to finally be getting some attention. I felt like Charlie getting the golden ticket in *Charlie and the Chocolate Factory*. In my mind, I was finally entering social acceptance and friendships.

Students gradually started asking me to do the cheers in the hallways and in classes apart from lunch. At first, Jacob came to my locker and asked, "Can you just stop it?!" It wasn't before long that he joined in with people asking me to do my cheers. The situation with the cheers came to a head during a football game.

In band class, we had an opportunity to do a color guard routine for a football game during half-time, and we only had little time to learn the routine. It was one heck of a workout on the arms. My mom came to video me, and after the performance, I hung around to watch some of the game myself. My mom was standing not too far away, putting her huge video camera back in its case. Then, a whole group of guys from school started to corner me and said, "Do your cheer, Sonia. Do it now." In unison, like a mantra, all the other guys in the group started saying, "Do it! Do it! Do it!"

People sitting in the bleachers nearby started to stare at me. My mom ran over and screamed, "Leave her alone! Do you hear? Leave her alone!"

They must not have suspected that anyone would come to my aid, and they left. We were both shaking.

Mom asked, "Sonia, what is this "Do it, Do it now?' What is it that they want you to do?" I tried to deny anything was happening to her out of fear of getting in trouble at home. She was smarter than to believe such a lie.

Mom called the assistant principal at the school that following Monday to report the incident. The assistant principal told her he would try to find out who the kids were, but he also told my mom that I enjoyed performing for people. He wasn't completely wrong because I was stuck in my fallacious belief that this was my golden ticket to friendships.

Naïvete is common among people on the autism spectrum due to their difficulty in picking up social cues. By the time a person realizes what the social cue is, it's already too late. I didn't realize that the social cue of laughter after performing the cheer was not positive. Hence, I already got stereotyped as 'the girl who would do anything,' the 'weirdo.'

Teachers started to intervene after the phone call to the assistant principal. My locker was located right down the hall from the special education room. I was in a modified special education program, so the teacher, Ms. Anderson, was aware of who I was. She and her paraprofessional, Mrs. Abignale, started to intervene first.

A couple of guys came to my locker and said, "Do your cheer, do it now." A whole group of people started gathering.

Mrs. Abignale approached the group and asked, "Is there a problem?" People left after that.

The second time this happened, she asked the guys if they would join her for a minute. I did not know what fully went on in the special education room, but through the side window near the door, I saw Ms. Anderson sitting on a stool, giving those guys a lecture. I came to find out that they were given detentions.

Oddly enough, before the teachers started to intervene, those boys used to sit and watch me perform the cheers from their lunchroom window. I caught a glimpse of them all staring at me one time. They looked at me as if I were some alien, and they saw all the laughter that ensued with groups of students crowding around. Nobody said or did anything. Sad that it took a phone call to the assistant principal for there to be some real action taken.

After a while, with enough interventions, people stopped asking me to perform, but the teasing and taunting grew. Pranks and spreading of false information to tarnish my reputation even further persisted. One such prank was that someone took my clothes out of my gym locker and switched them with another person. The gym teacher was the one who told me about it, but sure enough, classmates started spreading a rumor that I 'stole' someone else's gym clothes. It was then that I started to realize what harm had been done with all the cheers and how peers were capitalizing on all of it.

ANOTHER NEUROPSYCHOLOGICAL EXAM THAT INDICATED AUTISM SPECTRUM BUT STILL NO DIAGNOSIS

I started crying all the time at school. My mom already knew from the get-go that things weren't off to a great start. She used to make comments such as, "Sonu, you seem happier leaving school than when you go inside."

I used to deny anything was wrong at first out of fear. Before I went to Forest Ridge Middle School, my parents considered sending me to a small private school akin to St. Margaret's Academy. I detested that possibility because I was so jaded from what happened at St. Margaret's Academy that I would rather stick with the evil I knew.

The school made comments to my mother earlier on about my outbursts of tears and casual mentions of suicide before things got out of hand with the cheers. I was psychiatrically evaluated by a neuropsychologist in Dr. Kim's office, Dr. Marks, in October of 1994.

Dr. Marks was a soft-spoken gentleman who had to be in his mid-50s at best. He was well known throughout the area for being a very accredited neuropsychologist and a highly accomplished individual. I don't remember much about the neuropsychological exam apart from the fact that I was asked questions about sexual behaviors. I can understand why the questions were in there now, but back then I found it a bit perplexing. Throughout the exam, I recollect opening up to Dr. Marks about how I felt.

"Dr. Marks, I feel I have brain issues."

"What makes you say that?"

"I can't ever do anything right. School has always been a challenge for me, both academically and socially. I never was able to fit in with my peers. I was never treated well by teachers. I just can't seem to do anything right."

"Hmm, can you tell me more about that?"

"I think of suicide. I tell people about having thoughts of ending my life. I imagine at times how it would be if I was not here anymore."

"Why? That worries me."

I didn't have an answer to that question at that time. Now, I could say that I just wanted the pain to end, akin to how I wanted the pain to end the very first time I spoke about suicide on the camping field trip. I wanted people to treat me better, and I was embarrassed more than anything by another failed attempt at trying to make friends and be liked.

The results of the test were repetitive of what was shown when I was psychologically evaluated in early September of 1990 at the start of my second-grade redo. The exam results showed meltdowns and not understanding people's motives. The results showed developmental delay with regard to social development. These were all indicative of being on the autism spectrum. There was a paucity of information about high-functioning autism and what was formerly known as Asperger's Syndrome, at the time. The only way people understood autism was how it was presented in males. Hence, it's no surprise that many people thought about the movie *Rain Man* every time they even thought of the word 'autism.' Asperger's Syndrome, which was classified as higher-functioning autism, only came out in the DSM IV in 1994. The DSM stands for the *Book of Diagnostic and Statistical Manual* that mental health professionals use for diagnosing mental illnesses and developmental disorders in the hopes of being appropriately reimbursed by insurance companies.

The report referenced my conversation with Dr. Marks. He commented on suicide being 'a ploy for attention.' In retrospect, some of it was attention-seeking. The other was the depression and hurt speaking in loud volumes that fell on deaf ears.

JUMPING OUT OF A WINDOW, JUMPING OUT OF A CAR. FAKE ATTEMPTS

Fake suicide attempts started to become a topic at school. These suicide attempts were to compensate for my lack of ability to express what I was really feeling: embarrassment, shame, and the letdown for trying to be liked and accepted but failing at it.

The first 'attempt' that I told classmates was of me trying to jump out of my bedroom window. Students reported me to Mrs. Horowitz. She called my mother to come to her office for a meeting after school. My mom's car was parked in the front parking lot. I opened the door, got in the passenger seat, and reached over because I wanted to put the radio on. But I also wanted to know what would happen if I were to put the car in reverse because I was ignorant. I moved the gear, and the car started going backward. I started to panic because I couldn't stop the car. I threw open the door, jumped out of the car, and scraped up my knee quite badly. The car kept rolling backward, and I was screaming for help. The school nurse happened to be in her van to exit the parking lot. Another girl was sitting in her parent's car, watching the whole situation. We happened to make eye contact, and she had this look of disbelief coupled with "I want to die laughing right now."

The car continued to roll back into the school bushes. The school nurse said, "Go to the front office. They might be able to help you!" and drove off.

I went inside, and my mom was just walking around the main office with Mrs. Horowitz because their meeting was finished. I told them what just happened with the car.

"What?!" screamed the principal.

The principal, my mom, and Mrs. Horowitz went outside to check out the situation. After seeing that no real damage had been done to school property, my mom drove me home. One peculiar thing about the moment was that she never asked me what had happened or said anything about the meeting with Mrs. Horowitz. In retrospect, she was probably trying to process everything herself.

The next day, I told everybody at school that it was another suicide attempt. I had an entourage of people surrounding me and asking all kinds of questions akin to how news reporters try to ask questions to a suspect in a notorious court case.

"How fast was the car moving?" "Did you get hurt jumping out of the car?" "What happened to the car after?" "Was it damaged?" I heard people giggling as they were walking away. As much as I thought people were being entertained, people were also reporting this to Mrs. Horowitz. She called me to the office toward the end of the day and chastised me for telling people the fib. She told me that over 40 people had expressed concern about what was going on.

People told me off the following day at school for the fib. "You stretched the truth yesterday! What do you need? Some more attention?! Everybody knows you are doing this for attention!!"

The hurt got to a point that I wrote a note in science class that said, "I am just so tired of this all. I really don't want to commit suicide, but I feel myself just having to." The note got passed around, and there were some students who giggled at it. The note was given to the teacher. Students ambushed me all day moving forward. It got to a point where I told people at the end of school that I would go on my bike and ride myself into the middle of a busy street and end it right there and then.

KEY TAKEAWAY #1: Parents may want to consider having more open and honest conversations with their kids, especially when they notice they are not off to a great start at school. It might not hurt for parents to reinforce the idea of, "You can tell me whatever is bothering you, and you are not going to get in trouble. You are safe to tell me what is on your mind. I am not going to yell at you for your honesty with me." Once a kid knows they are safe, they are more likely to open up and be honest about what is happening.

KEY TAKEAWAY #2: Teacher bullying is not acceptable behavior. Parents need to be made aware of when teacher bullying is happening and have meetings with the school. Parents need to advocate on behalf of their child to ensure that they feel safe and supported when in the classroom. If there are issues that are frustrating the teacher, both the parents and the teacher need to be on the same page and work collaboratively to help fix the issue in an understanding and supportive way.

Perhaps, my parents could've had meetings with Mrs. Stephens alongside Mrs. Horowitz, and Ms. Anderson so that Mrs. Stephens could be aware of how she was coming across. Mrs. Stephens could've suggested ways to be clearer with her communication so that all classmates could have understood what the class was concentrating on. What we were learning in class could've been the main focus of tutoring instead of other subjects where I had relative ease.

KEY TAKEAWAY #3: Don't try so hard for people to like you. You don't need to act out in order for people to like you. In fact, trying too hard tends to do the exact opposite of what you are hoping for in that it pushes people further away. People who encourage you to act out or convince you to do things to put you at the center of negative attention aren't friends.

It is understandable to feel depressed when you are struggling to feel accepted and struggle to feel you belong. It is important for parents to also be aware of the struggle and continue to try to get the right help.

LEAVE OF ABSENCE

I was placed on a mandatory leave of absence. It was required that I undergo a psychiatric evaluation, and I was not allowed back into school until I was cleared by the psychiatrist. My parents met with Dr. Kim that same evening, and I was placed on leave. My mom told me before the meeting that there was a very real possibility that I might be admitted to an inpatient unit at a psychiatric hospital. Sure enough, Dr. Kim was strongly advocating that I be placed in a psychiatric inpatient unit.

My parents were vehemently against her advice. Dr. Kim kept saying, "Sonia should be in the hospital. There is no other way. Sonia needs to be in a unit. There is no other way."

I was petrified at what was happening. Out of the intense fear, I called

Lindsay because I wanted to share what was going on. She wasn't home when I called. I then remembered that she was at dance class with Jessica. Lindsay's mother asked if I wanted to leave Lindsay a message. I told her mother that I might be hospitalized. She seemed a bit concerned and asked me what was happening. I spilled everything out like an open book.

She seemed empathic on the phone. She thought the suicide stuff was just a mistake. "Sonia, I am sure what you did was just a series of mistakes. I am sure you won't do this again."

Luckily, my parents knew of another person through the Indian American society who practiced psychiatry. Dr. Patel had a practice in an office building across the hospital from where my parents worked. My parents had briefly met Dr. Patel at gatherings, and they had referred some patients to him in the past. Dr. Patel made an arrangement with my parents that he would evaluate me without placing me in the hospital.

When I first met him, Dr. Patel was very kind and sweet. Dr. Patel's voice was very gentle and soft, the softest I had ever heard in a male. He seemed like a guy I could trust based on his overall demeanor. One of the first questions he asked me was why I wanted to kill myself. I told him it was because Jacob didn't like me. That was the first answer I could think of. In retrospect, the story ran deeper than Jacob didn't like me. This had nothing to do with Jacob but everything to do with ME. It was too much for a 12-year-old to express, but all this pain had its roots starting from when I was 6 years old. Dr. Patel diagnosed me with major depression. I was given medications such as Prozac to help combat the depression. Every afternoon that week, Mom went to school to get my assignments on her way home from work. She found a lot of notes in my locker that I had written saying I was depressed. She found out from a teacher about a rumor that spread like wildfire around the school and became a hot topic among my classmates.

"Is your daughter okay?" the teacher asked my mom.

"My daughter is okay. Thank you for asking."

"I heard she was in the hospital."

"No, she is at home resting and working on getting better."

"Well, I just wanted to let you know that I heard she was in the hospital. I just wanted to see how things were going."

"I can assure you, after all, I am her mother; she is not in the hospital. Please feel free to share with whoever fed you that rumor. Have a good day!"

During the time off, Mrs. Goldstein, who was my fourth-grade teacher but became my tutor and eventually a very close friend of our family, continued her work with me during my leave of absence. There were a couple of days when my mom took me places to try to cheer me up. I went to one of my favorite museums: The Museum of Science and Industry. I thought it was a great way to continue learning even though I couldn't be in a school setting. The good thing about that museum was there were in-depth explanations of the exhibits, and seeing things illustrated helped me understand scientific concepts.

There was another evening when my mom took me shopping. In retrospect, I should've been in an intense therapy outpatient program during the two-week leave of absence. I could've learned some skills with emotion regulation and coping mechanisms. Some social and communication skills are addressed with DBT. Another option, a better option, was that I should've been sent to another therapist where I would have been seen at least twice to three times a week to work on social skills, processing emotions, processing my past, self-esteem building, and assertiveness training. Staying home without therapeutic interventions was not helpful or valuable.

I had a medication check-up with Dr. Patel before getting cleared to go back to school. Upon entering school, a lot of people were saying hello to me. I was immediately asked a lot of questions. "Sonia, how was it there? Were the other people scary? Are mental institutions really what they say they are? Did you meet any psychopaths?"

"What are you talking about? I was never in a mental institution. I was at home."

"Oh, we heard that you were in a mental institute. Hence, that was why you hadn't been in school."

The whole situation was infuriating because classmates such as Misty called me when I was home during my leave of absence. Yet, people thought it was fun to talk about how I was in a mental institute. When I tried addressing this issue with Mrs. Horowitz, she was anything but supportive.

"Let me ask you this, Sonia, what did you tell kids when you were sent home on your leave of absence?" Mrs. Horowitz questioned.

"People called when I was home, and I told them I was at home getting treated."

"No, you told students that you were going to a mental hospital, and you couldn't get out."

"I never said that. There were even people who knew I was at home."

"Sonia, you've said so many things to these kids. It's hard for me to believe that you never said a thing like that to them. Especially after you spoke of all those 'suicide attempts'. I want to let you know that you will NOT continue to discuss your condition with these kids. After all, they are here to learn. They are not here to listen to Sonia Chand's issues."

"I am not saying anything to them," I replied.

"I will see when it happens," she stated.

Chapter 4

NAVIGATING A NEW SYSTEM
OF RESTRICTION

TEACHERS ARE GOD, AND IT'S ALL YOUR FAULT. WE SHOULD SEND YOU AWAY!

The school had a meeting with my parents not too long after the leave of absence. During the meeting, the school told my parents that they would like to transfer me out of Forest Ridge School District and send me to a school for troubled children. It was the same school that students who get expelled from Forest Ridge School District were sent to.

The school had already made a file where someone had been observing and writing down my eccentric behaviors with the dates beside them. They told my parents that I was not Forest Ridge material because they didn't think I was intelligent enough. They said there was nobody else like me in that school to signify the extent of my eccentricity. My dad persistently beseeched the school to keep me for one more week. The school reluctantly agreed. This chapter will discuss more of the emotional regulation and coping skills I was forced to learn versus what more should have been done to ensure success from a social and emotional standpoint.

To say my mother was apoplectic when I came home after school that day would be an understatement. The thought of getting expelled from Forest Ridge was terrifying.

"Sonia, everybody kept complaining about you at the meeting. All your teachers had not a nice word to say about you! How can you do this?"

"I didn't do anything."

"What do you mean you didn't do anything? Don't you know that Papa had to beg the school to keep you for at least another week?! Every teacher complained that you are a problem in class. Did you know that there is no one like you at school?! If you get expelled from Forest Ridge, you might have to just stay home forever because I won't know what school to send you to, or I will send you away to India."

That only made me feel terrified and worse inside. The thought of being sent away— two continents across was scary. There used to be talks about sending me away to a boarding school in India when I was younger.

I used to be told by my parents, "Sending you to boarding school will really straighten you up."

What if I didn't need to be straightened? What if all I needed was to be the best crooked version of myself?

I didn't ask those questions at the time. However, I just knew going to India would've been the beginning of my end. If people in America were having issues with my peculiar behaviors, what on God's green Earth did my parents think was going to happen there?

It was bad enough that I couldn't even tell the people who were supposed to love me the most about what all happened that led up to these sixth-grade outbursts. The school had already written me off as being a 'problem child and attention seeker.'

I was being seen as the disobedient and defiant child at home. It was like I was under the eye of the perfect storm in the middle of the ocean in tumultuous waters. I tried to find solace that evening by going to my hip hop dance class. My mom's fury didn't cease while we were on the way to my class.

"You will not be allowed to listen to any music, let alone Indian music!"

"Why?"

"Let's get admission in a school first, okay?!!!!"

It wasn't as if not listening to music was going to cure everything. Ooooooooohhhh! In fact, music can be soothing, even if it is listening to classical tunes. I depended on music to help soothe me, and I used to like to listen to all kinds of music, including Bollywood music, even though I didn't understand the words.

Just because you take away a privilege, doesn't solve the issue at hand. The best way to get to the crux of the issue is to actually try to understand what is causing the outbursts in the first place, and intervene accordingly. A person who is acting out isn't necessarily doing so because of defiance, but rather, is asking for help, albeit in an unconventional manner.

NO SUICIDE CONTRACT SIGNATURE

The week in between the meetings, I couldn't keep my emotions to myself. I had to obtain another letter from Dr. Patel because I mentioned suicide again at school. Dr. Patel was lecturing me about my suicide talks, and all he was able to focus on was how the school wanted to expel me.

"Sonia, why do you keep saying that you want to kill yourself? They want to throw you out of school now."

"I have been trying to keep it together. I keep getting upset at school about how I am mistreated."

"But, now the school wants to throw you out. You need to try hard to not say that you want to kill yourself."

Dr. Patel printed out a 'No Suicide Contract.' Basically, it said, "I would not kill myself, or set it up so that someone else kills me for as long as I shall live."

I didn't think much of it when it was presented to me. I was told that we were in a 'crisis.' I didn't comprehend what that meant. All I knew was that things were starting to close in on me as far as tension, at home and at school. It felt as if the sun was setting and the darkness was about to fall, and I was blindfolded, navigating my way through the maze. This time, the sounds of others' footsteps were growing quieter and quieter in what almost felt like my own anxious breaths and footsteps were all that were left.

Our School is NOT for People Like You. You are Not Welcome Here

The second meeting occurred, and Dr. Patel attended the meeting alongside my parents. Before the second meeting, Dr. Patel switched my medication to Lithium. I had to take it twice a day: once in the morning at breakfast and the other at lunch time. I had to get blood drawn every two weeks to make sure the levels of Lithium were not causing irreparable harm to my body.

The school started the meeting aggressively. My parents and Dr. Patel shared what transpired at the meeting, and I also gathered information from what I read from the notes.

"Sonia needs to leave our school! She is not fit enough to be in our school, as we said last time. Dyers Village has a great school district that takes people like your daughter."

Dr. Patel advocated on my behalf.

"Hello, my name is Dr. Patel. I am Sonia's treating psychiatrist. I would like to say a few words. I recently changed Sonia's medication to Lithium which, in my professional opinion, will be very beneficial for her in helping her combat her moods. Sonia will do better if she is able to stay in an environment that she already knows versus having to start all over again. Sonia, obviously, has been through a lot this school year. If you throw her out, she will go downhill very quickly."

"Thank you, Dr. Patel! I understand your concern. However, Sonia is too much of a problem for our school. She annoys and upsets other students with her behaviors. Teachers aren't the most fond of her. She is a disruption to our school. We can't keep having this!"

"Let me assure you the medication and intense outpatient therapy I will do with Sonia will help. I have been in the practice of psychiatry for many years. If I felt that Sonia would do better at another school district based on my training and expertise, I would concur with you full heartedly. However, I strongly believe that the combination of medication and therapy will help Sonia immensely."

"I must say, we are definitely NOT happy about keeping Sonia in our school," said the school administrator. "Sonia doesn't belong here. Forest Ridge is for students who are intelligent, and she will be able to succeed not only academically, but in life."

"The way I see it, at the rate Sonia is going, I don't even think she will make it to eighth grade. I don't even think she will graduate high school or go to college. Forest Ridge is not the place for a girl like Sonia. This could all be so simple, and we can all peacefully end the meeting if you agree to send Sonia to the school we are recommending. We will even provide her the bus service from Forest Ridge to Dyers Village free of cost," said Mrs. Horowitz.

"Let's do this, before you make any drastic decisions on where to place Sonia, let's first see how she reacts to the new medication. I put Sonia on Lithium. She is instructed to take it every morning with breakfast. She will also take one dose at lunch. Sonia's family will provide the school nurse the medication bottle. Sonia will also see me on a weekly basis for outpatient individual therapy alongside medication management."

"Okay, we will honor Dr. Patel's suggestion. However, Sonia will have to be placed under restrictions in order to continue staying here. This means she will have very limited contact with others, and she will not be allowed to eat in the cafeteria. We will be keeping a very close eye on her. We are also changing her label so that she is identified as an 'emotionally handicapped' person. It is very clear that learning issues from ADHD and Learning Disabilities aren't the primary issue here. This must be agreed to in order for Sonia to continue attending school here."

"We agree," said my mother.

"Also, Sonia will need to maintain a certain GPA so she passes her classes with at least a 'C' or above. Otherwise, it would be best that Sonia leave this school."

"We agree," said my mother.

THE RESTRICTIONS ROUTINE

I had to report to the special education room, also known as the resource room, every day before school. I would have behavior reports from teachers that needed to be signed from a parent the night before and brought back to school each day. Failure to do so would result in having to stay in the resource room the entire day to work on class work. Ms. Anderson or her paraprofessionals were assigned to escort me to each class five minutes after the bell rang. Five minutes before a class was done with, I would have to be escorted out of class so that I am not in the hallways during passing periods. I had to go to Ms. Anderson's room to take my tests. During lunch time, I ate lunch in the resource room, and was escorted to the school nurse for my medication. After school, Ms. Anderson checked my notebook and made sure it was initialed by each teacher. Then, Ms. Anderson escorted me to the front to ensure I was picked up from school on time. The school's reason for isolating me in such a manner was that they wanted to 'take me off people's minds.'

If anything, what they implemented was antithetical to the goal the school was trying to accomplish. People used to notice me coming late to class and leaving early. People, including substitute teachers, used to make comments. "Why does Ms. Anderson have to come after you?"

Teachers didn't allow me to be in the classroom if they had to step out. I had to be watched as if I were a prisoner in a maximum-security facility. I remember clearly when our reading and English teacher had to make some copies of worksheets, she told me, in front of the class, "Sonia, I don't think I can leave you in here. You need to come with me." I got up and left with the teacher.

I saw the look on people's faces as I got up to leave with the teacher. They looked repulsed, and understandably so. After all, I wasn't able to make a good impression with the students, but now they are watching me get treated like a prisoner. The only crime I committed was trying to fit in and feel connected using what little tools I had in my toolbox.

HYSTERICAL LAUGHTER HE HE HA HA

The time I was eating lunch in the resource room could've been time spent working on building self-esteem, social skills training, and assertiveness skills with the school counselor, Ms. Sheldon. Instead, I would think of something funny and use hysterical laughter as a way to cope with a situation I resented being in. What made me even more resentful was I didn't always appreciate Ms. Anderson's demeanor. Ms. Anderson tended to be quite bossy and would constantly yell at students in the hallway. She was very quick to anger. It got to a point where I hated being around her and wanted to aggravate her as my way of acting vengeful.

I would think of clips I have seen in movies that made me laugh to no end. I would sometimes think of situations that wouldn't be funny to others, but would be to me. One was me bolting out of the resource room and running around the school with Ms. Anderson chasing me and tripping. The fall wouldn't be the hilarious part because the whole building would've probably shook as if we were in California during an earthquake. The funny part would be the look of shock on her face while staring at me with her mouth agape.

Getting under Ms. Anderson's skin seemed to work. Ms. Anderson was in the hallway speaking to a colleague and friend. The resource room was situated where the sixth graders' lockers were. You could hear people's conversations as they were gathering to get their lunches and put books away before heading to the cafeteria. That moment of just hearing others socializing, and my failed efforts that led to me being further isolated, made me feel an acute sense of sadness. I took it upon myself to start hysterically laughing away the pain. I laughed loud enough for people who weren't in the room to hear. Ms. Anderson then came into the room and yelled, "You will not embarrass me like that again!" Oh, I did not end there!

The last laugh occurred when Ms. Anderson didn't want me to speak much. She and her paraprofessionals were busy working on something. I continued to make conversation to annoy Ms. Anderson.

Ms. Anderson warned me, "Sonia, if you say one more word, we are all just going to get up and leave." I sure enough said one more word. Mrs. Anderson got up and said, "Come on ladies."

They all three left the room. The hysterical laughter lasted for at least 10 minutes solid. I kicked three adults out of their *own room*. In fact, I am laughing hysterically even while writing this, so much so that I was about to fall out of my chair.

Ms. Anderson had a conversation with a consultant after the incident. She was informed by the consultant to discuss my behavior with the principal and vice principal. He told her that she didn't need to 'take this from me.'

Ms. Anderson and I ended up having a conducive conversation about how we can be more civil. I agreed to try not to engage so much in hysterical laughter and be kinder to Ms. Anderson, mainly out of fear of getting into even hotter soup than I was already placed in.

MRS. HOROWITZ'S KEY PIECE OF EMOTIONAL REGULATION

Mrs. Horowitz also used to intervene to ensure that the restrictions were going smoothly. She used to reinforce that 'good behavior' was my key to more privileges, such as being allowed to go to a class without being escorted, or being able to sit in the cafeteria for lunch one day.

"What is good behavior?" I questioned.

"You do not cry at school, but rather go home and cry. Remember, people aren't here to listen to your problems."

"Okay, so how do I do that?"

"How do you do what?"

"How do I keep it in until I get home?"

This could've been an opportune moment for there to be some role plays, assertiveness training, and social skills training.

GRADING

1. Homework/class participation is a significant part of grade.

2. Student grades are based on content area.

3. Extra credit assignments to raise grade average if original assignments have been attempted.

er: Student will be escorted RC teacher between classes.
Lunchroom will not b allowed at this time.

Chapter 5

NAVIGATING RESTRICTIONS OUTSIDE SCHOOL AND CULTURAL BACKLASH

YOU'RE NOT FREE

The restrictions at school didn't only stay on school premises, but they carried to other areas, such as band concerts and the inability to attend the winter school dance. Because I was in the school band in sixth grade, it was a requirement for us to perform for the Winter Holiday Concert that was hosted in the Forest Ridge High School Auditorium. Both the middle and high schoolers were to perform their respective pieces. Ms. Anderson came to the band class and pulled me and a group of girls out. I was a bit perplexed as to why we were being pulled out of class.

"Hello, girls! I need you to do me a favor. I need you all to watch Sonia at this upcoming band concert. At the last band concert, parents complained that she was a distraction and disrespectful. We can't afford to have that happen again, as it is simply not fair to other students and their families."

"Okay," said the girls.

"If there are any problems, they must be reported."

"Okay," said the girls.

The girls that Ms. Anderson pulled out of class were members of the popular group. These were the only girls who seemed to give me some attention after everything, even though it wasn't sincere.

I wasn't sure what behaviors alarmed people at the fall band concert held in early October. I later found out from Dr. Shah, a therapist whom I saw briefly in high school, that people's parents instructed their kids to stay away from me. This would make complete sense as to why families complained to the school to try to preclude me from participating in the concert.

The fact that I had to be watched at a band concert, as if I were some prisoner in court in an orange jumpsuit in shackles awaiting a hearing from the judge was enough to make me upset. I broke down during the concert in tears while we were sitting and listening to the other bands perform. I just felt depressed that everyone else had friends and I was alone, and I felt embarrassed that I had to be placed in a situation where I had to be watched at all times. In retrospect, out of respect for my family and my feelings, the school should've just given me an 'A' for the semester in exchange for me not performing at the concert. It would've saved me the embarrassment and the undue burden placed on other students.

What I could've done differently at the band concert was try to just enjoy the music. It was hard watching everyone else bonding with their friends. I should've just tried to ignore what was happening around me as best as possible. Even though it was mandatory for all band students to stay throughout the entire concert, another option was to create an exception to the rule so I could've left after I was finished performing to save myself from getting upset and relieve others from having the undue burden of playing 'watch guard' on me.

INDIAN BACKLASH

The shunning and ostracism that took place were profound in the Indian American community. In some ways, I felt that from Dr. Patel when I would have my therapy sessions with him. He kept harping on the fact he had to advocate for me to stay at Forest Ridge School District. He very much resembled a parent scolding a child after the child had done something horribly wrong. It felt like he took on a family member role instead of an objective third-party person role that is expected of people in the mental health profession.

I thought he started treating me the way he did because we shared a similar cultural background. Dr. Patel behaved akin to the manner of many parents in the Indian community. Indian parents are not shy about giving unsolicited advice or putting their two cents into matters of others even though it's none of their business. Indian parents are quick to shame others who don't walk the straight and narrow. Moreover, they are quick to shame, especially women, whether their own daughter or someone else's, who have extra weight to them. The comments are relentless. Another reason to explain Dr. Patel's behavior was that he had a long standing financial connection to my parents for patient referrals. Hence, it was easier for boundaries to be blurred.

Throughout my time seeing Dr. Patel, he said only one thing that was something to ponder, "If you don't respect yourself, how do you expect others to respect you?"

It was a great question, undoubtedly. However, self-respect was what needed to be taught in therapy sessions through self-esteem-building exercises. Hence, while the concept of self-respect is valid and true, it's meaningless without having a sense of direction in how to attain self-respect.

Instead, all that was reiterated each session was, "When I went to your school, they wanted to throw you out that day. If I hadn't been there to advocate for you, that would've been the end of it as far as you attending school there."

This was anything but helpful. I didn't learn anything. The only thing that kept me at school that year was fear of my parents' wrath which would be sure to ensue if I got expelled and transferred.

KEY TAKEAWAY #1: It is important for mental health professionals to be mindful of how they talk to clients. Reinforcing how a clinician had to advocate for a client each session can come across as shaming. It is more helpful to focus on emotional regulation, conflict resolution, and social skills. Most importantly, it is imperative that a person on the autism spectrum be provided a safe place to fully be able to express themselves.

KEY TAKEAWAY #2: It is very common for individuals who have been bullied and faced peer rejection to have low self-esteem. Hence, if you are going to reinforce the valid concept of 'if you don't respect yourself, how can you expect others to respect you,' there needs to be direction provided on how to achieve self-respect.

HAPPY DIWALI. YOUR PLACE IS ON THE FLOOR IN THE CORNER

My parents were members of an Indian-American Physicians Group. The group was mainly composed of families living in or in the surrounding towns near Forest Ridge. Of the Indian people who attended the events, a good portion were those from my school. The people from my school had other friends from the surrounding towns because their families were friends.

People from my school already started giving me the cold shoulder early on at a prior event that the group hosted in the gymnasium at Forest Ridge Middle School. I remember trying to sit with classmates Amisha and Beena. Amisha was giving me the death stare, which I didn't pick up on at the time. Beena kept answers short with me and was trying to be somewhat polite. She didn't want to cause drama. Once Amisha got up, Beena followed suit.

I also saw another classmate, Leena, at the event, but she kept her distance from me. I can understand why people behaved the way they did. They were weirded out by my eccentric behaviors.

The experience I had from the event at the Forest Ridge Middle School gymnasium gave birth to the ensuing anxiety I started to feel about having to go to Indian gatherings thrown by the Indian American Physicians Group.

The next gathering was held at a community center in a suburb about a half-hour away from Forest Ridge. My mom was out of town that weekend to visit Jay in Virginia. He was away at school. I was left with my dad for the weekend. I knew my dad wouldn't allow me to not go to the Diwali event, especially because he told me that one of our family friends was joining.

The family friends whom he was referring to were the Ahujas. My parents got to know the family from working together at the same hospitals. The Ahujas were practically like family to us. The daughters were a bit older than me, and closer to Jay's age. I got along with both Ashima and Priyanka. I was open about what was going on with my mental health to Priyanka because she battled her own mental health challenges. I felt safe knowing she would be there, but part of me was anxious all day at the fact I had to attend uncomfortable cultural events.

My dad took me to a hairdresser earlier, as he saw a groomer in the same salon. I tried to calm my anxiety by getting a nice hairdo for the party. The hairdresser put some rollers in my hair that resulted in me having nice curls. It helped me feel somewhat better, but it didn't take away my anxiety. My dad assured me a few times that the Ahujas were coming and that Priyanka was coming with her parents.

However, when we got to the event, the parents told me that Priyanka wasn't coming. I tried to say hi to the people who were there. The people there were from my school and their friends from the neighboring towns. They barely acknowledged me and treated me as if I wasn't there. I was so lonely that I just sat on the floor in a corner in the hallway.

I understand that they didn't want to be around me because they got weirded out by all the acting out, and rumors spread. In all fairness, they were acting like a majority of my peers were; they didn't want me around and were embarrassed and ashamed to be around me. It just hit differently coming from a cultural community where you also feel othered and not welcomed. *If I am not even welcomed here, then where? Where else can I go to find acceptance and understanding?* The bitter truth was there was nowhere left to go.

I sat in the corner on the floor for a while. My dad was too busy socializing with his many friends and never once came out to check on me. I saw people giving me occasional glares when I glanced over to see what they were doing, but I just stared at the floor or the white wall across from me. The floor looked outdated and in need of remodeling. The floor had a color combination of white tiles with sprinkles of light blue tiles.

Only one girl, Nidhi, whom I met when I was younger at a family friend's gathering, approached me.

She said, "Sonia, people are feeling sorry for you because you are by yourself."

"They hate me, Nidhi."

"But I don't hate you. Why do they hate you?" Nidhi asked sympathetically.

"Because of everything that happened at school. Did they tell you?"

"No, they only said they were feeling sorry for you," Nidhi stated quite confoundingly.

"I went through a lot at school."

"Yeah, I am so sorry to hear that. I have to get going. We will catch up soon."

"Thank you for telling me you don't hate me. That means a lot."

"Aww, you are very welcome."

In all truthfulness, if people were really feeling sorry for me like they said they were, they could've easily taken the time to approach me and ask me to join. It's just that simple.

Sitting on the floor was only just the beginning of many Indian events I would be coerced to attend, where I was left to fend for myself. I eventually graduated from sitting on floors to sitting at tables alone. My butt felt happier on a chair, than a floor, screaming, "Please remodel me," after all. That was my only source of comfort for the duration of those parties.

People ignored me, akin to how I was treated at school. I only got into an incident one time that solidified how I was treated at these Indian events up until it was time for me to go to college.

THE BIG BLOW-UP

Ever since the Indian gathering where I was on the floor, I had bad feelings about having to attend such events on a much higher level. I would feel it in my gut because I knew I didn't fit in.

There was another stupid and senseless gathering in the spring of 1995. I wasn't looking forward to going, but this time, my whole family and a cousin were attending the event. When we got there, I noticed right away that Amisha and Beena were sitting at a table. I told my mom that people from my school were at the party. My mom thought it was important that I try to make friends despite the nasty way people responded before. She went to the table and asked Amisha and Beena if I could sit with them. They were polite to her, and they told her it would be fine.

Once my mom left to sit with my dad and their other friends at another table, things took a turn as could've been expected based on past behaviors. I was sitting next to Amisha and Beena's friend, someone who didn't go to the same school. I didn't know their friend all too well. I tried to get involved in the conversation, but I didn't have the appropriate skills to know how to join in an already existing conversation. Quite understandably, Amisha and Beena's friend got annoyed and made a snarky remark. That was when a full-out argument ensued. Amisha and Beena would laugh upon their friend's comments in support of her. They kept reiterating, "Stop, stop." We didn't stop that easily.

"I am trying to have a conversation with 'MY' friends. Who are you?" asked the friend in a snarky voice.

"I was just trying to be friendly and join in the conversation," I said rather timidly.

"You're really annoying. Leave us alone," she said in a stern manner.

"How am I the one being annoying?"

"The way you are acting. You won't even let us talk. Are you always this annoying?" she asked quite exasperatingly.

"I am not annoying."

"Sonia, you weren't even invited to sit here. Your mom had to come and ask," said their friend.

"So?" I replied.

"My point exactly. You know, why don't you name your friends or count how many friends you have. I bet you don't have many."

"I do. In fact, I am throwing a huge birthday party for when I turn 13," I stated quite adamantly yet with deep sadness, because her words about me not having many friends cut deep.

"I bet nobody will even show up," said their snarky friend.

That was enough to get me to leave the table. Amisha, Beena, and their friend all gave me dirty glares as I got up. I heard laughter as I was walking away. I ran into Nisha, a friend whom I had met during my second-grade redo. I had no idea she was at the gathering. I told her about what happened. She told me how she thought Amisha, Beena, and their friend were really nice. Nisha came to find out their version of the story from them. I would come to learn years later that those girls called me a 'bitch' behind my back. I would rather be called a 'bitch' than a baby, so in my mind, that was an improvement.

Chapter 6

NAVIGATING RESTRICTION
ADJUSTMENTS

RESTRICTION ADJUSTMENTS, A NEW CRUSH, DESPERATION TO BELONG

Towards the end of sixth grade, I was allowed to invite a classmate to come and eat lunch with me in the resource room. I was only allowed to invite females, and I was not allowed to invite Kiera. Ms. Anderson and Mrs. Horowitz thought she was a bad influence and, overall, bad news. At first, I didn't understand why they felt the way they did about her, but I would eventually learn as middle school went on. The invitations had to be made through Ms. Anderson or her paraprofessionals, and they would be the ones to extend the invitations. I just had to provide the names to either her or the other two ladies first thing that morning.

Inviting someone to lunch was a challenge because so many of the kids were turned off by my behavior. The only people who were giving me attention were people in the 'in crowd' in what would be insincere ways.

There was a reason as to why the 'in crowd' kids were nice. It was because they wanted to come and see what my house looked like. At a certain point in sixth grade, Blossom suddenly started to become very nice to me, alongside Kiera and their friend Emilie. They would call me on the phone. I didn't catch it at the time, but the phone conversations consisted of either Kiera wanting to know if Blossom said anything about her or vice versa. Hence, I was being used as a g- between. This is where people on the autism spectrum tend to trip up by not understanding subtleties to know what is happening in a conversation and understand motive and intent. Hence, understanding social cues through social skills training is very important, especially since a majority of communication is non-verbal and contains subtle nuances that one needs to understand.

Emilie was also a sixth grader at Forest Ridge Middle School, and I was introduced to her over the phone on a three-way call. There were plenty of people whom I didn't get to meet due to the fact I was under restriction. Emilie asked me about the rumors that went around the school and about the crush on Jacob. She seemed very nice at first.

The Super Bowl was around the corner, and my parents used to like to host Super Bowl parties. Sure enough, I told Kiera, Blossom, and Emilie about the party, and they agreed to come. When they came, they behaved in a way that caused my mom concern. My mom didn't particularly care for the way they ran all over the house. They were acting like many of the people who had come over before….treat the house like a museum and forget about the person who invited them. Safe to say, that was the only time they came over until I threw my final birthday party. Invitations were never reciprocal.

Also, those girls were aware that I wasn't in good standing with my peers at school. It was their opportunity to take advantage and come see the house. The only other time someone came to my house was before the spring dance. I was on the phone with Sheila after school and asked her if she had plans before the spring school dance. She told me she had no plans before the school dance. Well, before I could finish asking her to come over, my mom grabbed the phone from me and asked Sheila. That was not a good move on my mom's part because learning to invite people should've been a skill I practiced.

A major lesson I learned is that if people are suddenly being nice to you when they haven't been, know that it is for a reason. Usually, they want to get something out of you. People will usually tell on themselves by letting out subtle cues. An example would be "What did she say about me?" as illustrated by Blossom and Kiera.

This chapter will discuss more important lessons of self-advocacy, such as coming to grips with handling others and dealing with getting into trouble due to behaviors encouraged by others. I will share what I know now that I wish I had known back then.

LUNCHROOM CONVERSATIONS

When people came to the room, all conversations were monitored to make sure I didn't say 'anything inappropriate.' I tried to keep conversations simple and let them do more of the talking. In retrospect, a lot of conversations centered around guys. I needed more conversation skills, for sure. There were times when I would ask people a lot of questions about their dating life, as I found it to be quite intriguing that they were able to get dates and have guys like them.

There was one conversation where I asked a lot of questions to someone about her dating history. I asked her about her past boyfriends. She was not rude about it, and she answered the questions. I didn't realize I was coming across as nosy until Ms. Anderson pointed it out after lunch was over.

What could've been fun and unique was if Ms. Anderson or her paraprofessionals had assigned me a conversation prompt to practice during lunch every day for a week before assigning a new conversation starter. This would've not only taught social skills but also been more tailored towards evaluating and giving constructive feedback in a productive way.

HELLO ANDREW, YOU'RE MY NEW CRUSH. DO YOU WANT TO BE MY BOYFRIEND?

Seventh grade allowed me a little more freedom in that I was able to go to classes and my locker on my own. I still had to report to the resource room in between classes, but I didn't have to be escorted by the special education teacher or her paraprofessionals. This would become important as things played out that year.

Everyone was required to take social science in seventh grade. The class was only a semester long. Paradoxically, the class was about things such as peer pressure, self-esteem, how to handle conflict, and navigating social issues. Topics were touched on a very surface level. On the first day of class, we had to come up with a word that described ourselves using a letter that started with our first name. I came up with 'Sweet' Sonia. I heard some chuckles but I never picked up on what exactly was so funny. Upon introduction, I started to notice Awesome Andrew.

The desks were arranged in a horseshoe shape in rows that covered the room. Andrew sat across from me, and he was in clear view. I sat in front of Jacob's good friend Mike. Mike and I just started discussing one day about crushes in general. Mike said with everything, there is always a 50% chance. Mike asked me who I thought was cute in seventh grade because Jacob was out of the question. I told him I thought Andrew was cute. Without my permission, Mike suddenly asked Andrew if he would go out with me. Andrew, without even thinking for a second, said "no".

Like Jacob, Andrew was not very easy to forget about right away. I tried to at least be on good terms with Andrew in a friendly manner. Andrew was only nice when he had to be, such as when we all had to work together on an in-class assignment. Outside of that, Andrew did not want anything to do with me. I used to call him at his house, and he told me not to call him anymore, even after having a few phone conversations with me. I should've respected his wishes sooner. I was just desperate for acceptance and for someone to think I was cool. I was looking for answers on what I needed to do to change my whole being.

Students learned quickly that reporting me to people like Ms. Anderson or Mrs. Horowitz was the weapon they needed to get me into any kind of trouble. After all, they had great visual examples of me being escorted and kept away from others. My annoying behaviors and desperation pushed things to a point where Andrew would put his middle finger up at me every time our eyes made contact, and he would even whisper "fuck you" to me every time he saw me in class.

BULLYING TO THE NEXT LEVEL

The restrictions clearly failed to accomplish any purpose of getting me to act 'normal.' My desperation morphed from throwing birthday parties as a way to win over friends to having full-on acting-out routines at school. I was practicing the exact definition of insanity, doing the same thing repeatedly, expecting to get a different result. I didn't have any other skills, and I was using my pain from rejection by peers and even Andrew to act out as a way to cope and try to get acceptance in ways I knew how. I would voluntarily make a weird noise or say something off the wall with peculiar body gestures. Other times and often, other peers would prompt me to act up.

A prime example of acting out happened during the Halloween school dance. The past couple of weeks leading up to the dance, people kept telling me to dye my hair bleach blonde or shave my head. In fact, the girls even got Andrew to stand with them while they were telling me to take such actions one day after school. The ideas came about when I asked the girls how I could look better. I was looking for any kind of clue that would lead me to the correct path in this maze.

To quiet people down, I told them I was going to dye my hair bleach blonde. When I got to the school dance, the girls were waiting by the entrance to see if I had my hair dyed. They all laughed when I didn't.

The lights dimmed, and the music started playing to kick off the dance. It was not long before a group of popular upperclassmen started screaming my name to grab attention from everyone else. Before I knew it, I was in the middle of the dance floor with people circling around. I was doing dance moves that were accompanied by an uproar of laughter. People started egging me on by mocking moves to get me to go again, and the cycle repeated itself for at least a good 25 minutes before being pulled out by a teacher. It got to a point where even the other tutor that my parents hired for me for 'extra help' asked me with a negative connotation, "Sonia, what were you doing at the school dance? Fifty people told me that you were dancing away." I didn't realize I was getting set up until it was already too late.

My own behaviors often caused the ridicule and derision I faced from peers. Dances, funny noises and songs, and weird faces became the new repertoire for performances. The so-called 'friends' who used to be nice in front of Ms. Anderson and her paraprofessionals showed great discomfort to have me at their table when it was my day to eat in the cafeteria.

The girls would sit closer together next to one another and create distance from me. They would sometimes join in the taunting and teasing along with the guys. One instance stood out clearly: I was standing outside to get fresh air after eating lunch. A group of eighth graders thought it would be fun to play the game 'monkey in the middle' but with a twist. They took the ball and threw it in a way that it would continuously hit my head before I even had a chance to catch it. Before I knew it, the ball was picked up, and I would be hit again. People all stood around and laughed as if they were watching some comedy movie. I told the teacher, who happened to be my social studies teacher, about the situation. He told me I needed to address that elsewhere, even though he was on supervision duty for lunch. It was his job to make sure things were smooth and people were behaving. Hitting a girl with a ball repeatedly while people stood around and laughed is not a good example of things going smoothly.

What would've been a good comeback to those guys was to catch the ball if I could and then throw it hard at them. I mean, if they were strong enough to hit a girl on the head with a ball, they could handle a good throwing of the ball from a girl.

KEY TAKEAWAY #1: It is important for educators to be aware of reported bullying that is taking place and do something about it. If a teacher is on supervision duty, it's the teacher's job to walk around and see that things are going smoothly. A ball repeatedly hitting someone in the head is an example of things not going smoothly.

If a student tells a teacher about a bullying incident, it's the teacher's job to take the incident seriously and act. Don't just pass the puck to someone else; do your job, especially if it is your job to supervise.

KEY TAKEAWAY #2: Bullying has evolved with technology, as people now have access to phones with cameras. Thank goodness social media and smartphones weren't in our lexicon when I was growing up and going to school. Social media posts are rampant, especially among teenagers. It would behoove parents to inquire about policies that the school has for social media, phone usage, and bullying.

KEY TAKEAWAY #3: Be honest with what is going on with peers to the people who are supposed to 'help you.' If you are not being treated well, try to find ways to get yourself out of a situation by either finding another table to sit at, even if by yourself, or staying away from people who treat you poorly.

STIMMING

Group work was another opportunity where others felt discomfort and embarrassment. Oftentimes, teachers ignored the laughter. If they intervened, it was only done half-hazardly. People used to laugh when the teacher would announce the groups and my name was called. An instance that stood out was science class. I was assigned to work with Misty on a class assignment. People were paired in groups of two. Misty had the most uncomfortable look as if she were about to become sick to her stomach and hurl at any moment. I was stimming by rocking because it was self-soothing.

Stimming is considered a self-stimulation behavior that is often used for self-soothing.[1] In fact, stimming is a notable symptom of an autism diagnosis.[2] Stimming behaviors take place in many different forms.[3] These include, but are not limited to, hand flapping, spinning in circles, finger flicking, rocking, pacing, echolalia (where words and phrases are repeated), humming, blinking, and the use of objects such as flicking a light switch on and off; or, opening and shutting doors.[4]

My stim of choice was rocking. Rocking acted as a replacement for the swings, and just the motion of back and forth was calming. It reminded me of a rocking chair that my aunt and uncle had when I was a kid, and my grandparents used to sit on that chair. It was one of the few happy childhood memories I had.

Even though I was rocking as a way to get through being in a toxic environment, other kids weren't able to see rocking as anything but another way to bully me. What was ironic about the situation was I wasn't

---

1   *American Psychiatric Association (2020, December 7) Understanding Stimming: Repetitive Behaviors with a Purpose.*https://www.psychiatry.org/News-room/APA-Blogs/Understand-Stimming-Repetitive-Behaviors-Purpose

2   Id.

3   Rudy, L.J (2024, August 18). *Examples of Stimming.* https://www.verywellhealth.com/what-is-stimming-in-autism-260034

4   Id.

intentionally trying to act out. People were mocking the move, and one classmate was encouraging others to join in the bullying. I got defensive and told people to stop. I saw Misty mocking me by making a face and saying, "Stop." This only encouraged others to continue doing what they were doing. I was flabbergasted the most by Misty because I never thought she would've stooped to that level.

Even though it is hard to completely stop the stimming, having other tools to handle situations would've come in handy. I should've told Misty that her behavior wasn't called for, and if things escalated more, perhaps let the teacher intervene. As for the kids mocking the stimming, I could've just pretended not to listen or see and just concentrated on getting the work done we were assigned.

FROM MATH CLASS TO THE ASSISTANT PRINCIPAL'S OFFICE

Math class was the epitome of where I was seen as 'the problem.' The teacher, Ms. Morgan, was a rather elderly woman in her mid to late 60s going into her 70s. It had been rumored that she taught at Forest Ridge Middle School for the better part of 50 years. She had quite a hunchback and was made fun of quite a bit by other students for being old and senile. Ms. Morgan lectured only to the bare minimum that she could. We would start every class by reading aloud the answers to math problems. If someone didn't get the problem right, she just moved on to the next person who could give the correct answer. Math class was mainly busy work that she assigned us to do during class. There were students who mouthed off or acted like smart aleck to Ms. Morgan, but she would just tell them to "be quiet" or sometimes bicker back. She never tolerated any of my behaviors.

Emilie was seated two rows across from me and in the front row. She would often bug me to make a silly face or do a silly gesture. Her requests were most often made when Ms. Morgan's back was turned, and she was somewhat relentless in asking me to do things. I would act up to stop being asked and be left alone. This wasn't the correct way to respond. If I had known back then what I know now, I would've been persistent in saying "no." This way, I could've saved myself from a lot of trouble.

Emilie had a unique, hideous laugh—not quite the hyena type of laugh, but hideous enough that it stood out. Ms. Morgan used to automatically kick me out upon hearing Emilie laugh without even seeing or knowing what happened.

Emilie's laugh, to the teacher, was like what Pavlov's dogs were to the sound of the bell. As Pavlov's dogs learned to salivate with the sound of the bell, the teacher learned to automatically kick me out of class by the sound of Emilie's laugh. I was sent to the resource room upon getting kicked out each time. I would act out even more in retaliation for getting kicked out of class due to frustration and embarrassment. I would start laughing out loud upon leaving the class, which, in turn, encouraged the class to laugh.

There were times when I would skip down the hallway and sing loudly, "We're off to see the Wizard, the wonderful Wizard of Oz." The class laughed even harder upon hearing that. The frequency of how much I was getting kicked out of class only increased as the year went along. It started coming to a head towards the end of the year.

Ms. Anderson got sick of me always being sent to her room. I ended up being sent to the assistant principal's office twice. The first time, I was let go. I should've taken that opportunity to explain the situation to the assistant principal, even if that meant telling on myself, too. Perhaps the situation in class could've been handled better if the assistant principal had intervened and told the teacher the full story of what was happening. This could've possibly avoided me having to be sent down a second time, which I was. The second time, I wasn't so lucky. Coincidentally, Ms. Anderson was at the office and had just gotten off the phone with my mom regarding summer school options.

Ms. Anderson started to describe my situation in math class. Mr. Benson didn't have any interest in hearing what Ms. Anderson had to say. He was more concerned about yelling at me, the 'problem child.' After all, that was how Mr. Benson used to show his power—his strong temper and bad attitude toward students at large.

"If you can't behave properly in that class, I am going to call your father and have him take you home for five days. Is that clear?!" he exclaimed.

Ms. Anderson tried to explain to him again about what was going on in math class. Mr. Benson blatantly told Ms. Anderson that he didn't care to hear it. This goes to show how much a person on the autism spectrum can be easily targeted and scapegoated for things.

The first thing Ms. Morgan told me in class the next day was, "Sonia, remember what Mr. Benson said. Five days."

She started keeping a closer eye on Emilie, something she should've been doing a long time ago. Emilie tried her best to get me to act out. Ms. Morgan told Emilie to leave me alone. She had to say this at least a few times before Emilie got the message.

SWIM UNIT TIME—WATCH WHERE YOU MOVE

Towards the end of the year, as part of gym class, we had to complete a swimming unit. I was not savvy like the other girls who knew how to cover themselves better when changing out of their clothes and into their swimsuits. All it took was someone to ask me to step out of the way in the locker room for a rumor to circulate around the whole school that I walked around the locker room naked. I constantly received comments from sixth, seventh, and eighth graders throughout the day. "Sonia, I heard you were walking around naked in the locker room. Are you a lesbian? Why were you walking around naked in the locker room?" Each time a comment was made, it was accompanied by immediate laughter from others.

I was ambushed by girls during gym class. One classmate screamed loud enough for everyone to hear, "Maybe we can get someone to walk around naked in the locker room like Sonia."

I stood up for myself and told her I didn't do that.

"Sonia, it's true. Ask anybody in here," she stated.

It was radio silent in the locker room. The only conversation I heard was when people were lining up to go to the door, only to say, "It's not a rumor; it's true."

Upon seeing me, another classmate came up to me and told me I had to cover up more when I was changing. This was followed by an uproar of laughter from other classmates.

The laughter and derogatory comments continued, and it was relentless. "So, Sonia, naked walker in the locker room, huh?! "Locker rooms are for changing clothes, not for walking around naked. You should know this by now. You're a seventh grader!." "Why were you walking around naked? Do you like some girl in class?" All the teasing and taunting I faced throughout the whole day made me quite upset. I had to be escorted out of my reading class and taken to the resource room because I was in tears.

I brought my concern to Mrs. Horowitz. The first time, she told me that I needed to stop crying about the rumor. She noticed my crying increased and was calling it out. It took me being persistent for Mrs. Horowitz to take charge of the situation because she was acting quite lazy. I knew if nothing was done about it, it would only get worse.

Mrs. Horowitz called several classmates to her office. Between each one telling on the other, Mrs. Horowitz would leave the office to let the secretary know to call the next person down. Those girls took the moments Mrs. Horowitz was out of the office as a way to discuss whom not to tell on. Eventually, the person who started the rumor was discovered: Donna.

Donna was part of the middle group on the social hierarchy. She was well-liked by many classmates, and she was respected by the popular kids.

When Donna was asked about what happened in the locker room, she said, "I saw Sonia standing undressed in the locker room while everyone else was changing. She was moving to the end of the aisle of lockers undressed."

"Do you know why Sonia did that?" asked Mrs. Horowitz.

"No," Donna said.

"So, in other words, you started the rumor about Sonia walking around naked?" asked Mrs. Horowitz.

"Yes," said Donna quite timidly.

"Do you know the rumor about Sonia is all over the school now, and she is getting harassed by both girls and boys for it?!" asked Mrs. Horowitz in a somewhat stern manner.

"Yes," said Donna.

"You wouldn't want me to call your mother about this, would you?" Mrs. Horowitz asked.

"No," said Donna.

"Here is how we will handle this situation: You need to tell people who bring up the rumor that it isn't true. The only reason you saw what you saw is because people asked Sonia to move out of the way," Mrs. Horowitz instructed Donna.

Mrs. Horowitz had Donna practice the script with her. Just like that, the meeting was over. Mrs. Horowitz kept some of the other girls back post-meeting to teach me how they stayed covered up while they were changing out of clothes. They just spoke about how they wore longer shirts that helped make it easier for them to keep covered. Mrs. Horowitz then explained to the girls how convenient Donna was already dismissed from the meeting by then, about how I didn't know this skill. This was Mrs. Horowitz's attempt to make herself look and feel accomplished, knowing full well she just allowed a bully a slap on the wrist.

Even though the outcome of the meeting wasn't the greatest, I was proud of myself for being persistent. I didn't realize at the time that I had some inner strength and courage to not only endure all the challenges emotionally and socially, even though I perpetuated a lot of the struggles myself, but the persistence to finally have the guidance counselor intervene based on my own inner drive to not give up. This is something I can say I am proud of myself for.

Chapter 7

SUMMER OF A LONELY AWAKENING

BELOW AVERAGE SOCIAL SKILLS

At the annual end-of-year case conference meeting, one of the things most harped on by teachers in their reports to be shared at the meeting was my social skills. Teachers commented on my peculiar behaviors, and they perfectly characterized my social skills as 'below average.' Apart from being 'below average,' teachers noted the desperation for acceptance. The teachers were correct! My Social Science teacher put in her report that "Sonia tries too hard to get people to like her." My reading teacher even noted how I was the target of cruel jokes and peer ridicule in the hallways.

However, the school administrator just read through the reports as if they were reading an article from *Time Magazine.* There was no further discussion on what the next steps would be in that area in terms of how I would be helped as part of my Individual Educational Plan. Instead, the school decided to take me completely off restrictions for the eighth-grade year. In my mind at the time, I wasn't bothered one way or another.

At the case conference meetings, if teachers comment on your kid's poor social skills, it is in the parent's best interest to ask more questions and be proactive in working with the school to address the social skills and how things will be handled in the next academic year. That is one thing I wish my parents were educated on when going to the case conference meetings.

SUMMER OF LONELINESS, AWAKENINGS, AND FAILURE TO BE A FRIEND

It finally clicked in the summer of 1996 that none of my efforts to make friends worked. I was rejected, and understandably so, by these so-called 'friends.' Every time I tried to ask people to do something, the answer was always, "I can't." It wasn't much different from previous summers with peers, especially in elementary school when classmates would say "I can't, I can't" when asked to do things. However, this summer, it hit differently. I think the realization that I tried too hard to make friends to have it be a fiasco and the realization of all past failures with friendships came crashing down like a never-ending tidal wave.

One evening during the summer, I was on the phone with a classmate, Eileen, "Sonia, you should know a lot of people hate you." This was not new knowledge, as I had been told on numerous occasions by various people, including Misty, that "a lot of people make fun of you."

Funny fact, Eileen used to laugh with others who set me up, and she would play both sides. On the one hand, she tried to show everyone she was with the pack by engaging in laughter and, at times, participating in setting me up to act out in gym class. Other times, she would tell me how 'disruptive' I was with her friend Brittany. They were also friends with Emilie.

"I am not a weirdo," I protested.

"Yes, you are! I heard about things you used to do in sixth grade, even. I heard about all your crying outbursts. I also heard about those cheers. That was all really stupid. You are weird!"

"Who hates me?" I asked.

"I better not tell you because you will cry forever."

"Okay, I guess I am hated then," I said despondently.

"Yep!"

"Bye." I hung up the phone.

Eileen was telling the truth and sealing the lid on what everyone was thinking. Also, Eileen gave an important social cue: to give up on even trying to be her or other people's friend. Eileen said how a lot of people hate me because I'm annoying and weird, and calling me annoying and weird was her way of saying, "I don't really like you either." I didn't catch it at the time.

My parents took me to a new psychiatrist during the summer at a major teaching hospital in Chicago. At first, I was hesitant to go because of what I had seen happen with Dr. Patel. My mom was insistent that I see Dr. Wagner because they automatically thought of him as good because of his position at an acclaimed teaching hospital. I would come to learn that just because someone is a physician at an acclaimed hospital doesn't mean they are a good fit with a patient. My parents sat with me in the first session, and Dr. Wagner got a good history of things that have transpired thus far. Dr. Wagner sold me on, "Let's work on getting you some friends." I was desperate to learn how to be successful socially and how to not always be the one targeted and set up for cruel jokes, needless to say, targeted for peer ridicule and derision.

En route to the hospital, my parents asked me if I was planning on throwing a birthday party that year. I told them, "No." This was the first time I was vulnerable around them, and told them, "Nobody will come, at least not for the right reasons."

"Why don't you think they will come?"

"Because they have been blowing me off this whole time. We are into August now. Nobody wants to hang out with me. People keep telling me,

'I can't, I can't, I can't.' There's simply no need for a birthday party."

This was the first time I was honest and outspoken. This was the first moment I felt brave and was proud of myself for a short moment. I had to learn this lesson later due to the fact that I spent a summer vacation visiting relatives abroad the year prior.

My dad insisted that I try to make friends with his colleague's daughters. He was alluding to the same girls whom I didn't get along with before at Indian events. I told him "no," especially after how they acted at Indian gatherings. It wasn't easy for my family to understand why I was having social issues, and it would remain that way for a long time.

MEETING MEERA AND AMBIKA

Outside of school, my family was part of an Indian cultural group. This consisted of more down-to-earth families. The families lived in neighboring townships and suburbs in both Illinois and Indiana. Some of the families we already knew from having lived in Forest Green and Forest Ridge, but there were new families we met. I connected with Meera the most. Meera was a year older than I, and she lived in the neighboring township of Oakland. Meera was quite mature for a 14-year-old. The way she carried herself was somewhat atypical of what one would see for an adolescent, particularly around adults.

Unlike other kids and teenagers who were interested in bonding and hanging out with people of their respective age groups, Meera was more interested in helping the Aunties (Indian people call the elderly Aunty and Uncle, respectively) in the kitchen.

When she hung out with the rest of us, Meera was quite fun. She had a very kind personality and an open vibe about her. In October of 1995, a group of us performed a skit together for a Diwali show that the group put on and rented out a recreation room for. Our friendship started to grow slowly after the Diwali performance.

I saw Meera again when Ambika, another girl from the cultural group, had a birthday party with her friends and invited Meera and me. Ambika was similar to Meera in that they were both very ambitious-driven, culturally oriented even more than I was, excelled both academically and in sports, and were very well-liked by their peers. Ambika lived in Dyers Village, and she was a year younger than me.

Ambika had a youthful glow and a bubbly personality. One of my favorite memories of her was when she used to try to sing along to popular pop songs, but she wouldn't know the lyrics and just make up her own. We would all get a good laugh out of it.

It wasn't shocking that Ambika had tons of friends at her birthday party, and they were all spending the night. They were all youthful and bubbly as well. I could also see a stark difference in people in terms of the energy I was able to pick up from Ambika and her friends versus people from Forest Ridge. For one thing, Dyers Village was a much bigger township. There was much more diversity in terms of people's socioeconomic makeup. Places like Dyers Village didn't push an 'elitist' attitude in the same way Forest Ridge pushed it. Hence, there was a more relaxed energy from people from places like Dyers Village because the pressure to live up simply wasn't there in quite the same way.

During the birthday party, everybody got along. I noticed that even though the girls were pranking the cute guys in their grade, they weren't making prank calls in the same way that people did when they came to my house. The difference was that people were laughing with Ambika and making sure she was included. They didn't just help themselves to the phone or anything at the house.

Throughout the party, I noticed that Meera wasn't really connecting with many of the girls. She and I sat on the couch in Ambika's basement and chatted. This was where I learned more about Meera and her strong interest in dancing and tennis. Our love for dancing and music connected us.

Ambika and Meera were family friends, and it felt weird to be invited by Meera to get together to do something without families connecting. Ambika and her family ended up moving to India for her father's sabbatical at the beginning of the summer of 1996. Her father was a professor in electrical engineering, and he had been assigned to teach at a university in India for at least one year. I felt sad to see Ambika and her family go, and I missed them dearly.

FAILING TO BE A FRIEND. THE PROBLEM WAS ME!

The first time Meera came over, we watched a couple of movies and ate some dinner. I learned more about Meera's childhood and her friends. I started getting together with Meera more towards the end of the school year and into the summer. However, my lack of knowing how to even be a friend, alongside the challenging year I had with the bullying and hard attempts to fit in, precluded me from being able to be a good friend at all.

In fact, if anything, I WAS A TOXIC PERSON. I WAS THE PROBLEM. I HATED MYSELF AND TURNED ALL OF THE NEGATIVE MESSAGES FROM OTHERS INWARD SO THAT I WOULD HATE ME, TOO! THIS IS WHAT MADE ME TOXIC! I didn't quite realize how negative I became until moments would come up over the summer when I would start berating myself in front of Meera.

When I say 'berate myself,' I mean I would say the meanest things about myself to myself. I would call myself 'trash, junk, unworthy, stupid, scum,' etc. I was desperate to feel cared about and accepted and for someone to actually show me how I was wrong.

The only way I felt I could be proven wrong was if people from my school came around and said, "Sonia is cool and worthy of being around and wasn't worthy all the bullying. We are sorry you went through that."

I also was looking for an answer to the main question of "why?" "Why was it okay to always target me?" "What was in it for everyone to laugh at me and not like me?"

What I didn't realize was this was an internal job and that it was my responsibility to validate myself. This was where attending therapy sessions and even going to supportive group therapy where social, emotional, self-esteem-building, and communication skills were taught.

There were times I cried to people like my mom and even Meera about all the bullying and how I was friendless at school. There were times when I had fun with Meera. I learned how to do some of the Indian dance moves; we would watch fun movies together, and we would even go and play on the tennis court. Despite the validation Meera tried to give me in letting me know that I wasn't trash, I was dying inside. I was depressed and anxious about having to go back to the same place where I was broken down so badly. I would have to go back to the place where I was left friendless and lonely.

I started to feel the pain in my body. My stomach used to hurt every day. I knew it was due to emotional pain rather than any physical ailment based on my intuition back then. The constant self-deprecating dialogue where I told myself on repeat all day long that "you are trash, nobody likes you, you were and are never invited by people at school to anything, everybody thinks you're a baby and a weirdo, nobody really likes you, and nobody will ever be your friend," certainly didn't help.

I couldn't appreciate the good times as much as I should've. If I could've rewound time, I would've appreciated all the good times I had with Meera instead of constantly getting down on myself. I would've taken notice of the fact that SOMEONE WAS ACTUALLY TRYING TO BE MY FRIEND! However, all I could focus on was everything that happened during school, with all the alienation, ostracism, and bullying. It was all that I could talk about, and that was all I could perseverate on. Meera, understandably, grew tired of it.

I can't help but look back and feel ashamed of myself for how I handled the friendship situation with Meera.

Meera and I remained close for a little bit at the beginning of the academic year. She eventually distanced herself from me. I remember trying to discuss with her about how I noticed how we weren't hanging out much on weekends like we used to. All she said was, "You have to understand my situation. I am busy with school."

I respected her decision. I would see her sporadically at the cultural group meetings my parents and I went to. Meera already had plenty of other friends from her school by then.

What made the friendship break even more saddening was Meera was my only friend. Now, that was gone, and it was my fault. I wrote to her years later apologizing for my behavior, and she was very sweet about the letter. She denied that I had anything to do with the friendship breaking, which was a generous lie on her behalf. I knew what I had done, and even though I regret the way I treated Meera at the time, I have learned to have compassion for myself and forgive myself for not knowing any better at the time.

KEY TAKEAWAY #1: Even if you have been going through a tough time being bullied, if someone shows you friendship, please try to relish the moment. Friendships thrive when both people are happy and can do fun things together. Friendships don't thrive when one person is always negative and talking about their issues.

KEY TAKEAWAY #2: Bullies want you to feel bad about yourself as part of their scheme to exert power and control over you. Please remember that the messages they give you are lies to make you feel bad.

Chapter 8

SOCIAL SKILLS AND ACADEMIC WINS

YOU GO FIRST

It's not surprising that in the first week of school, the same girls who blew me off all summer kept asking me if I would have a birthday party. They seemed to remember how, last school year, I had a birthday party the first weekend of school. People were 'nice' on my birthday and sang 'Happy Birthday' at school. They kept asking me if I was going to have a birthday party that day and if they would be invited to the house. I told them, "I was not." After all, if they could blow me off all summer, they don't deserve access to my house. A good life lesson to remember is that people who weren't there for you during your struggles don't deserve a spot in your celebrations.

Dr. Wagner gave me some good advice at the beginning of eighth grade. "The next time someone tries to set you up to act weird, you tell them, 'I will go after you go first.' That way, you let them be the ones doing the acting."

"What happens after they are done?" I asked, bewildered.

"You tell them, 'I changed my mind. But, it looks great on you, so keep on going.'"

"Oh," I replied.

"Don't allow these kids to put you in a position where you get set up," said Dr. Wagner adamantly.

Sure enough, after the girls were done singing, they tried to set me up to act out. I acted out once at the beginning of eighth grade. It took just one more name-calling of 'weird' and remembering Dr. Wagner's advice to finally quit with the repertoire. The refusals of acting out weren't received well. Everyone kept asking, "What's wrong?" What was wrong was that I got a clue and was not entertaining people at my own expense anymore.

Bullying persisted for a bit in the last year of middle school, but after it was handled, people just completely left me alone and ignored me. The loneliness came on strong, not to say it didn't while I was acting out. In fact, I used to cry a lot at school and used to express to people that I didn't have any friends. I cried to family members too. I was comforted by an uncle who used to just say that kids could be very cruel. Somehow, hearing that was soothing. By the time I was in my last year of middle school, the crying morphed into Friday nights and weekends crying at home because I had no friends.

While I was acting out the previous academic years, everybody else was able to form strong friendship groups. By the time I realized all how the combination of acting out and the bullying from others affected my ability to really bond with anybody, it was too late. People had already formed their friendships, and they were miles ahead in the maze. Loneliness was acute during passing periods and lunch. In those moments in the cafeteria, I missed eating lunch in the resource room. At least, even if I didn't have a peer to eat with, I was still around people. At times, I started missing being on restrictions and being escorted to classes.

I continued taking dance classes for a little bit as a way to find comfort and relief from the everyday throws of being in a horrible environment, but the homework overtook me in eighth grade and precluded me from having an outlet.

Mrs. Goldstein took notice of how much work I had to do, and she used to ask, "Does everybody have this much homework every night?"

I didn't know about everybody, but I was up to my eyes in homework each night; let alone the periodic exams.

So, remember how my parents were told, "Sonia would be lucky to make it to eighth grade?" Well, not only did I prove the school wrong by making it to eighth grade, but I did one better: I MADE THE HONOR ROLL FOR THE VERY FIRST TIME EVER. I had no idea that I had made the honor roll until Ms. Anderson told me the day report cards came out. Later that day, after school, I didn't have to tell my mom because Mrs. Horowitz already called her to tell her the news. We celebrated by getting ice cream.

Mrs. Goldstein couldn't contain her excitement about me making the honor roll, either. She just kept asking, the most excited I have ever seen her, "Did you really?! Did you really?!" Her face just lit up the entire room.

The next day, during study hall, all the students who made the honor roll were recognized by their study hall teacher in front of the class. They also received a pencil and a certificate. I remember when my name was called, and I heard people say "Sonia?" in a bewildered tone amongst each other with their friend groups. I am sure everybody was rather flabbergasted upon hearing my name getting recognized for the Honor Roll. After all, it was not every day that you heard someone's name who was considered a "problem child," "unfit to attend a 4-star school district," and "unlikely to make it to eighth grade, let alone high school" make the Honor Roll.

What made the victory even sweeter was that people like Jessica saw me get my award. I remember Jay told me, "Sonia, you know you just told your school 'fuck you,' right?"

He was right. What a classy way to say that, too!!!

Chapter 9

HELL AWAITS

THE BIG LET DOWN

My mom eventually gave me some hope when she said we would move to another area outside of Forest Ridge. Both my parents got on board eventually, but more so, my mom was on board to let me have a fresh start somewhere else.

Weekends used to consist of looking at new houses and visiting the schools in the neighborhoods where we were looking. I started using my weekends to imagine what high school could be like. I saw houses and envisioned having a fresh start, making good grades, and perhaps being involved in some extracurricular activities where I made friends. Most importantly, I would have a clean slate without judgment and stereotypes.

At the core, I was a nerd. I loved to learn. As I kept maturing and growing into my own, my goals and aspirations changed as to how I saw myself in the future. I went from dreaming about being a famous dancer to becoming a doctor.

I used to take the high school courses handbooks from the schools I visited and read the course descriptions. I used to imagine what courses I would want to take while I was at school and just imagined the people I would meet. I envisioned people coming over to the house on a Friday night or weekend or me going over there.

I thought I had it figured out. I thought if all I did was not talk about myself much, not act up, and just pretend to be like everyone else, that would be the golden ticket to acceptance and friendship. Lo and behold, there was much more than what meets the eye.

I thought we would have a place settled, and my heart got set on a school in the suburbs of Chicago. I told people I was moving away out of my excitement of the prospect of moving, irrespective of whether they wanted to hear it. Of course, people didn't really care. eighth-grade graduation rolled around before I knew it. The graduation ceremony was held during the day at the Forest Ridge High School gymnasium. The gymnasium at the middle school was under construction at the time. As we walked to the gym, Emilie came up to me and wanted me to break into a dance on stage during the eighth-grade ceremony.

"Sonia, you should totally go out with a bang! When you get on stage, you should just be like 'time out. I think you all should just check out my dance!'" Emilie started doing some arm pump moves in an attempt to incite me to do something wildly foolish.

"I can't do that. I will get into major trouble," I said, quite taken aback.

"Oh, come on, Sonia! You're not even going to be at our school next year!" said another classmate.

"No, thank you! I can't get in trouble."

"Sonia, you could be the Urban Legend of Forest Ridge if you did that dance. It would be one for the records," said Emilie.

"I can't get into trouble."

The excitement of graduation ended with me finding out that the move wasn't going to happen after all. My parents decided that the bidding for the houses wasn't worth it, and the commute would've been too much of a hassle. Now, onto the additional four years of Forest Ridge Hell I went.

Chapter 10

STAND UP FOR YOURSELF

DR. SHAH, I NEED HELP!

My mom found me a new therapist at the beginning of freshman year to help me navigate through the beginning of high school. Forest Ridge High School was predominantly made up of the same people who attended Forest Ridge Middle School. There were very few new people, and the people who were 'new' had attended St. Joseph's Catholic School, which was only Kindergarten through eighth grade.

A lot of the kids already knew each other due to community sports and church memberships. By the time freshman year started, everybody was well integrated with their friend groups. One of my parents' biggest fears was a behavioral outburst repeat of sixth grade, and this was a fear they held onto for all the years while I circumstantially matriculated in Forest Ridge School District. My mom ensured that I saw a therapist right away for that reason.

Upon meeting Dr. Shah, I thought she was very attuned to how I was presenting and was sharp at picking up my peculiarities right away. One of the first things Dr. Shah noticed was delayed social skills akin to those of my peers. She also pointed out that my facial expressions were different and awkward throughout the course of the conversation. Dr. Shah mentioned a lack of eye contact.

Dr. Shah also taught me some social skills, such as how to stand up to people at school if they started bullying or harassing me again. "You have to put people in their place," she said. "If someone is being rude to you, then give them a double dose of what they've given you. Let them have it! No one should treat people that way. And when you stand up for yourself, they won't."

Her idea made me smile, but I didn't know if I could do it. To avoid getting picked on, I would try.

I took Dr. Shah's advice very literally, as is typical for someone who is on the autism spectrum. If I thought people were teasing me or making fun of me, I got very defensive and snappy, and nowhere did this happen more than in our ultra-competitive gym class. Other people paired up in teams of two for the pickleball unit, whereas I was solo. I was playing against Misty's team.

I wasn't the most coordinated or athletic. I would miss the ball quite frequently and was slow to move. I would hear comments from not only Misty but others on the tennis courts. "You couldn't hit that ball? Can't you move any faster? Pick up the damn ball, and *hurry up!!*"

That really irritated me, and I told people to "shut up" and "fuck off."

Finally, as we left the court, Misty tried to be nice. "That was fun. We should do that again."

I remembered what Dr. Shah taught me. I had to stick up for myself. I did not like how Missy was being so snippy the entire time. I told her, "You were being so rude, and now you are being so nice. What is your scenario?" This phrase was exactly what Dr. Shah taught me to say.

Missy said, "Excuse me, but you told me to fuck off."

Misty went around saying, "Sonia is such a trip," laughing about it with other girls.

I didn't think anything was funny. I turned to a classmate in our gym class who was from a different grade and told her, "Some freshman girls are just bitches."

Another classmate happened to overhear me and turned towards me, and said, "You're a bitch, too, because you're a freshman." Then, she went to others and told them, "Sonia said you're bitches because you're freshmen," but that was not what I said. Those other girls started giving me deadly stares. People kept away. I was confused. I simply thought I had been sticking up for myself.

I talked to Dr. Shah about the situation. She said, "It's good not to be too over-eager or too nice at school, but Sonia, you have to be careful about name-calling."

I took part of her advice to heart. I ignored people who I thought were fake, such as the popular girls, but I never really understood the reasoning behind not retorting to name-calling if I felt attacked.

Gym class remained a challenge when it came to changing clothes. During dodgeball and soccer units, the teacher would have one team turn their gym shirt to distinguish between the teams. The very first time the teacher gave the order, I didn't do it because I was afraid of being laughed at. I didn't know how to turn my shirt around in the way other girls were able to turn theirs without their bra showing. I eventually complied the next time we played soccer in gym class so as to not be seen as defiant. I couldn't do it without showing my bra, and soon enough, people started to notice. I was observant of the fact that girls' eyes used to wander during the times when people were turning their shirts around. I used to be weirded out by it because I never understood the point of watching others turn their shirts around.

I overheard a conversation in which that became a topic of discussion. Of course, with that, the past about middle school swimming unit locker room drama came up. The guys who overheard it did not even attend the same middle school.

Spanish class was another place where I would show my snappy and defensive side. I scolded a classmate for repeatedly calling me "Sanya" after I corrected her on how to pronounce my name. She continued to then call me "Sanya" in a sardonic tone. I told her I was not going to answer her. This caused her to laugh and become defensive herself. She exclaimed loudly to other people she was sitting by, "Sonia just gets worked up over nothing."

I followed what Dr. Shah taught me in the hopes that people would learn to respect me. If anything, what I was getting was antithetical to respect. I was made more the prey for the pariahs.

How I should've handled the situation was to say something back in a way that wasn't defensive. Maybe I could've tried to go along with it and mispronounced her name in the same joking manner. I could've maybe said, "Who is Sanya?"

It became a weekly event where I would call Dr. Shah on Friday, crying out of loneliness. I felt all alone and alienated at school every day. I used to sit by myself at tables during lunch, and then I would sit by myself in the Hangout Area once I finished eating. I used to either do homework or watch people socialize with the aim of learning skills.

Dr. Shah had me read this book about friendships, which spoke of learning hobbies, dressing nicely, and being interesting so that people would want to be interested in you. I didn't have hobbies by the time freshman year rolled around. In retrospect, I didn't even know what I was good at or what would interest me. I had no idea who I even was, and my self-concept never really had a chance to develop or be explored.

Dr. Shah gave a recommendation to my parents that I learn a sport. She introduced us to the Love All Tennis Club in a nearby town, about a 15-minute drive from Forest Ridge. In fact, Dr. Shah knew one of the tennis instructors well because he used to give lessons to her family. I grew to take a liking to tennis, and eventually, tennis would become my anchor to get through high school.

Dr. Shah emphasized the importance of trying to make friends outside of school. I took her advice and went to a Halloween Party at a place called the After School Center. Dr. Shah had to insist that I go there a few times. I finally agreed because it was for Halloween. After all, who doesn't like some good candy or Halloween-themed desserts? The person in charge of the program, Ruth, had spoken to Dr. Shah before and was informed to come and find me.

Ruth was dressed as the wicked witch from *The Wizard of Oz.* Her excitement in welcoming me to the place was refreshing. There were a lot of activities going on. In one room, people were watching scary movies. In the other room, which was a gymnasium, there were people who were dancing, and the remainder of the people were sitting on the bleachers.

Once I had finished touring the place, Ruth introduced me to one of the girls, who then took me to the bleachers. I was introduced to more girls. They were speaking about how they wanted to beat up someone who was in attendance that night. I was immediately turned off by the conversation. I didn't know how to leave, and in an attempt to divert myself from the negativity, I tried to have a conversation with the person sitting next to me.

The conversation started out intense. She automatically started telling me about how she wanted to drop out of school because she was doing really bad. I tried to ask about the extracurriculars she was part of as a way to try to change the tone of the conversation. She told me she used to play softball. She then went back to the other conversation where the girls were still talking about wanting to gang up on another girl. Safe to say, I got up and left the place altogether. Thank goodness my dad and brother stuck around to watch the scary movies in the other room. I later found out that the After School center was for at-risk youth to keep them off the streets. From what I heard of that conversation that night at the Halloween party, it made complete and utter sense.

The next place I tried to make friends was the Hindu Temple, which was about an hour away from Forest Ridge. I signed up to take two classes: Bhagavad Gita and Hindi. When I first got to the Bhagavad Gita class, people were very welcoming. I ended up striking up a good conversation with one person in particular, Bhavna.

We ate lunch together after class in the temple cafeteria. We bonded over TV shows, movies, and tennis. We exchanged numbers and even had a phone conversation after my second time attending the religious class. Bhavna and I discussed making plans to get together after temple and go shopping. I thought I was making progress. I couldn't have been more wrong.

The next time I attended Bhagavad Gita class, I was treated as if I had done something horrible that would cause her to be angry with me. I noticed Bhavna didn't acknowledge me at all. When I tried to talk to her during a break between classes, Bhavna blew me off and continued a conversation with her friend. Her friend gave me a look of sympathy. I left feeling bewildered. Bhavna behaved standoffish the next weekend, too. I never found out what happened. The first automatic thought that came to my mind was 'another friendship failure to happen yet again.' After all, it was easy to assume the problem was me because of the relentless social challenges I had.

Furthermore, it is easy for people on the autism spectrum to believe that every rejection or mistreatment by others is about them or something they said or did. However, that isn't always the case. Sometimes, it's about the other person and the shortcomings that person has.

After that, I didn't bother to continue going to the classes. I figured that if I was going to have to be driven that far to just be treated poorly, I already was dealing with it enough. I deserved better.

Chapter 11

ZARA AND DR. SHAH FALLING OUT

Towards the end of freshman year, Dr. Shah did something a bit peculiar that went beyond the scope of her practice: she spoke with Zara about *me*. Zara was a very well-liked fellow classmate. She had a very charismatic and outgoing personality, and she had many friends in both the popular and middle social groups. Dr. Shah told me of the conversation she had.

"I spoke with Zara about you."

"Okay."

"She said to me, 'Sonia doesn't talk to anybody at school.'"

"I caught her up to speed about everything that has happened and what your situation was and is."

"Zara then told me that she was inundated with stories of the behaviors you used to do in sixth and seventh grade. She was in agreement with what you had mentioned before, that you thought people should just see you for who you are today instead of judging you based on your past. She also told me that she had defended you behind your back this year when people were saying things about you with another classmate."

"Oh. I had no idea someone stood up for me."

"Zara said she stood up for you to three girls who were not saying the nicest of things about you. Perhaps you should try to talk to Zara at school."

"Okay."

I said hi to Zara in the hallway when I saw her, and it was a quick hello kind of thing. Lo and behold, Dr. Shah had another conversation with Zara. They came to some agreement that Zara would befriend me. I believe this was Dr. Shah's last-ditch effort because she didn't know what else to do to help me. There was probably ego at play because she was, after all, a *doctor* of psychology, and it would've been a big blow to her to say, "I don't know how to help you anymore," or "How I can be of support to you?" However, this doesn't excuse unethical behavior, such as breaking the confidence of a client and going outside professional boundaries to facilitate friendships.

I got a call from Dr. Shah on a Saturday morning out of the blue. Dr. Shah told me, "Sonia, you need to give Zara a call. I am going to give you her number. She said to call her this afternoon around 1:00 p.m., and she will take you shopping."

At 1:00 p.m. sharp, I called Zara. I told her that I spoke with Dr. Shah, and she gave me the number. Zara was excited to be on the phone, and I went to her house later that afternoon. We ordered a pizza and watched the movie Scream.

After that, Zara called to ask me if her family and my family could hang out.

"Sonia, my parents would like to set up a meeting with your parents. I come from a very conservative family, and my parents won't allow me to hang out with someone whom my parents don't know."

"I get that. My parents are the same way in that they would rather know more about the families of people I spend time with," I responded.

"Okay, cool. Could you and your parents come over to our house on Sunday afternoon?" Zara asked

"I don't think that should be an issue. Let me check with my parents and call you back."

Zara's parents and my parents ended up meeting briefly over a weekend. The connection between the parents happened rather quickly. We threw a milestone birthday party for my uncle. Zara's parents and siblings all came to the party. Zara's elder sister went to the office room and got on the phone the whole time. I happened to go to the office room to check on Zara's sister, as she had been in there for quite some time. Her sister looked startled and just asked, "Nobody can hear me, can they?"

"No," I said, rather puzzled.

"Oh, okay. Good. Also, nobody is going to use the phone, are they?"

"No," I responded.

"Oh, thank you," she said with a sigh of relief.

I just left the room. I had an intuitive sense that she was talking to a guy her parents might not have approved of.

After only a little time with Zara and her family getting to know us, they did something that took me by surprise. My parents and I went to her house to have dinner one Sunday evening. I was taken by surprise when I was informed that their family bought us a kitten. We had never expressed to them about wanting a pet kitten, as we already had pets. As much as I was shocked by the gesture, we politely declined to take the kitten. Even though I found it odd that we were offered a kitten as a present, I couldn't quite put my finger on what was odd about it.

My parents later told me about Zara's parents talking about their own healthcare business. They were indirectly looking to my parents to refer them to potential patients. Hence, it all made sense: 'We will try to lure you into a business deal with the simple gesture of giving you a kitten.' Hence, this was a major clue that the friendship with Zara was part of a much bigger scheme, and it was not altruistic. It also has me wondering how much of a cut Dr. Shah may have been promised from any potential business deals.

The times Zara and I hung out were some good times. We watched movies and TV shows and had good laughs. There were other times, though, when it was challenging. Zara used to ask often about my past.

"Why did you do those dances and faces, etc., for people?"

"Because I was trying to make friends."

"Why did you talk about suicide?"

"I really don't want to get into it."

"Just one more question, was it true about the car and the mental institute?"

"I really don't want to talk about it."

"Just answer this."

"No, I was not in a mental institute. I spoke about suicide because I was depressed."

This conversation would happen a few times throughout the friendship. Dr. Shah eventually intervened and told Zara to back off from asking about the past. This was something I should've been taught to do for myself instead.

At times, Zara would make comments about wanting to include me in her friend circle, but she wanted to make sure people didn't feel 'uncomfortable.' She would tell me things such as, "People think it's weird that I let you into my conversations."

Those were not things I needed to hear about, as they were triggering for me. I already struggled with low self-esteem and lack of self-worth, so comments like that were like rubbing salt in the wound.

Zara would go on to tell me about how people would say things like, "That was some crazy shit Sonia did, and she deserves to be punished for it."

How ignorant! As if restrictions and being treated like a prisoner in street clothes weren't enough punishment right?! I didn't have the skills to tell Zara, "I would rather not hear things like that from you because it doesn't make me feel good." I should've stood up for myself, but I was afraid of losing a friend. If a friend is truly a real friend, that person will respect the boundary you put up. If not, then the person was never a true friend to begin with.

As the 'friendship' with Zara went on, she and her family would give more clues that they wanted something. Zara would make comments about my family regarding money. There was also a time when her mother asked why my parents weren't sending her patients for her healthcare business.

I started noticing weird behavior during summer school when Zara would hang out with her sister and their friends. They would stay away from me at school. I expressed this concern to Dr. Shah, and she immediately gave me some blowback. "What, Zara can't have any other friends? That is really unfair of you, Sonia!" Zara would give Dr. Shah feedback on how I interacted with others at school.

The bullying picked up during class breaks. Cody, a classmate, used to ask, "Sonia, do I turn you on?" All the while, he would make inappropriate gestures. Girls would sit around and laugh. I was confused as to what was so funny. He used to do it often, and girls laughed as if it never got old. At times, he would ask if I was trying out for cheerleading because 'I would look good in the skirt.' That would cause even more laughter from girls. I used to laugh with them as a coping mechanism. Zara complained about that to Dr. Shah. Dr. Shah told me not to do that next time.

A good response to Cody would've been, "Was that supposed to be funny?" or "Where is the punchline?" That would've put him in his place quickly. Also, optimistically, this could've shut the girls up, too.

I was successful at putting one person in his place. One morning before school, another classmate, Corey, tried to have a go at me. He asked if I liked some guy who attended the school. My gut instinct told me not to give in and say 'yes' because I would have been laughed at.

Corey was also friends with Cody and the rest and the other girls who used to get amused by Cody's lame jokes. I told him, "No."

Corey started to have a go with me by asking me, "Why not? He isn't doing anything to you, so why don't you like him?"

I tried to ignore him when he struck me with, "It's people like you that ruin this world."

I told him, "Thank you," and didn't give him the satisfaction of letting him know he hurt my feelings by his comment.

A way I could've handled it was to say, "It takes one to know one." I just wish I was more socially savvy to know how to handle snarkiness with matching snarkiness.

What was also jarring was the therapeutic relationship I had with Dr. Shah, which was starting to be contentious. For one thing, she was obtaining feedback from Zara, which indicated that the friendship wasn't working. Zara wasn't the only person whom Dr. Shah was talking about me with in my school.

Dr. Shah used to talk about how she had other classmates of mine who were her patients. She never divulged their names, but they knew I was her patient. She used to also tell me what they would say about me, such as having bad posture and not dressing up to what they thought were their standards. The fact that my name was brought up and discussed in somebody else's session, knowing that I was a patient of Dr. Shah, was completely unethical and, needless to say, unprofessional.

Dr. Shah's use of "pay attention to students who might start being nice to you" as giveaway clues to who is seeing her as a client was unprofessional.

Dr. Shah used to get upset with the never-ending desire I had for friendships and connections. Friendships and how people connect to one another became an intense interest for me. Dr. Shah used to say, "Develop other hobbies and find more concrete goals."

I tried to keep occupied with tennis even though I wasn't as athletically gifted as others. I liked the challenge of trying to improve on something that didn't come easy to see how far I could get. After all, this theme of having to improve to see how far I can achieve has been a remnant throughout my life, especially up to that point.

The same dreams that I used to have in middle school about becoming a famous dancer now transferred to becoming a famous tennis player. This was all rooted out of loneliness, ostracism, lack of self-worth, and bullying. I invested my free time and energy in trying to improve my game after having an illusion of such a dream when I wasn't studying.

I tried to take a drama class at the beginning of my sophomore year, but I figured it would be too stressful to have to memorize verbatim lines and show emotion. It was my own insecurity and fear that held me back. I should've tried other activities apart from tennis. In the worst-case scenario, it might not have worked out. In the best-case scenario, I would've fallen in love with another hobby.

THE FALLING OUT

Zara and I's friendship came to an end at the start of sophomore year. Things started to happen that stood out more. My mom organized a small birthday gathering with family and friends. Zara was invited to the birthday, but she never showed up or called to let us know she wasn't coming.

Zara and I shared a class together, and the bullying was quite noticeable. People would make snarky remarks when I would answer a question in class or participate. I just asked to leave class one day because I didn't feel like being in that environment. I wanted better. My classmates thought I left because I couldn't handle them. Zara told me that the whole class made fun of me for not being able to 'take the bullying.' Nobody should ever have to 'take the bullying.' Instead, people should be given the skills to learn how to handle such situations when they come up so that others know that this person is not to be bullied.

Zara thought I had too many insecurities. She was not wrong. Some of my insecurities were that I needed to put my foot down and not allow negative talk from people who claimed to be my friends. I also needed to learn to love myself and be my own friend, but I didn't know how to do that.

I have said negative things about myself in therapy with Dr. Shah, and I got shamed for it rather than worked through with it.

"How dare you say that about yourself? It only shames a person even more than they are already shaming themselves."

If a person speaks negatively about themselves, there usually is a reason. It's not necessarily always attention seeking, but rather an underlying message that a person is carrying around a lot of pain. It also tells of a person's negative core belief about themself, and that negative core belief which is learned somewhere along the line. My negative self-belief started as a young child and only grew because of the reinforcement of such beliefs through various circumstances and encounters. It's like watering a plant; the same way plants grow with proper hydration. Negative beliefs can also grow with proper reinforcement.

Dr. Shah and I subsequently had a falling out after I had to be sent to her when I had a meltdown at school. My mom attended with me and sat quietly as Dr. Shah called my behavior attention-seeking. She accused me of talking about suicide to Zara, which I never did. She brought up past friendships, such as Meera's, that failed.

"You want people to fix you and treat your friends like your therapists. You want people to feel sorry for you. You want people to say, 'Oh, Sonia, I'm so sorry.' That's not how this works. You need to stop with this nonsense NOW! Do you understand?!"

"No, I don't treat my friends like therapists."

"Yes, you do. Look at what happened with Zara and even Meera."

"Zara just didn't want to be my friend anymore."

"That's because her mom is saying 'no.' You said you wanted to kill yourself to Zara, and even her mother got scared."

"I never said that."

"Look what happened to Meera. You did the same thing there. Poor Meera, honestly!"

I started stimming and shaking my legs up and down during the session. Dr. Shah started noticing. She said, "Stop it!"

"Stop what?"

"Stop with your leg."

I started again with the opposite leg. She and my mom laughed. I lashed out and called her a 'bitch.' Yes, I know it was rude and inappropriate, but she irked me during that session.

She went on to say, "I can do this because you can't take it." She was alluding to the bullying she was doing and was well aware of it. She was using her attitude and power to feel better about her own shortcomings as a clinical psychologist. Bullying a teenager as an adult once again shows unprofessionalism and a lack of class and dignity for the other person. I felt like a witness on the stand being chewed up during cross-examination.

"I want to kill myself!" I exclaimed out of frustration and anger.

"Go ahead, go kill yourself," said Dr. Shah. Such appropriate advice coming from a therapist, right?! (insert sarcasm).

"The next time you make a scene at school, you will never be allowed back here. And one last thing, the way you behaved, you're not worthy of friendship."

This statement stuck with me for a long time and only reinforced, *"Sonia, you are a piece of unworthy trash nobody likes."*

I had already made up my mind that I would never see this woman again.

Chapter 12

MAZE TAKES A NEW DIRECTION

At last, the 1998-1999 sophomore academic year, more like surviving boot camp, came to an end. That year seemed to drag, and I was numbed out emotionally for the remainder of that year. Academically, I struggled. It was no lie when they said, "Sophomore year is the toughest."

I was happy to have passed my classes and been promoted to junior year, even though my grades weren't as high as they were in freshman year. I helped Mrs. Goldstein with her summer school class for three days when it first started as her volunteer assistant to help out with group activities. I ended up leaving to go on a week's trip to Boston, and I would return only to stay a short time before spending the rest of the summer in Virginia.

My cousin Raju and his wife Radha were living in downtown Boston. In February of 1999, my mom's side of the family had a reunion. A majority of the family came, with the exception of a couple of my cousins. In retrospect, the reunion happened at a perfect time because this would end up being the last time my grandma would see my mom and all her siblings together. Amongst the cousins in attendance were Raju and Radha, and it was planned that I would come to visit them for a week when school let out at the end of the academic year.

While I was in Boston, I fell in love with the city. Who knew that years later, I would come to dream of qualifying for the Boston Marathon and crossing the finish on the infamous Boylston Street? It still hasn't happened yet, but I am keeping hope alive. If I am still given the gift of aging like fine wine, I hope time qualifying standards can start to be more in my favor.

While it didn't dawn on me to see the finish line on Boylston Street, I got to explore areas of Boston. I went to Freedom Trail, walked on the path near the Charles River, and saw touristy spots such as where the *Cheers* bar was located. I loved the ambiance of Boston, and I thought to myself that I wouldn't mind living in Boston one day. In fact, my heart always had a soft spot for the East Coast, and I would eventually live out East for five years in the Big Apple.

While in Boston, I got a makeover. I had my eyebrows waxed for the very first time. Radha took me to get my hair done and styled, akin to Jennifer Aniston's classic hairstyle on Friends in the '90s. I didn't quite understand, and it would take me years to learn that in order to upkeep a good haircut and style, it would take me practicing with sectioning the hair properly and blowing out sections in pieces. This also required lots of practice. It would take me until I was in my upper 30s to finally grasp how to blow out my hair on my own.

While we were out and about, Radha took me shopping and helped me pick out a cute outfit. It was a cute pink button-down blouse with a long black skirt. I also bought matching accessories. Before I boarded the plane to head home, Radha touched up my hair, and we put on the outfit with makeup.

My parents were astonished at the makeover I had upon seeing me come off the airplane. Pre-9/11, parents were able to go to the gate and pick up their kids. I could see in their eyes that they were stunned at the change. I will say that getting a makeover and seeing how I looked after was the first time I actually liked and appreciated how I looked for the first time in a long time. Thank you, Radha!!

SUMMER OF 1999 IN VIRGINIA

The idea of spending the summer in Virginia came about when my dad's youngest brother flew into Chicago to attend a prayer service held for my grandmother. Later, when we were sitting in the study room, my uncle asked me, "Sonia, what do you have planned for the summer? It's right around the corner, you know."

"I have nothing special planned. I'll probably go to summer school and take some courses to keep busy and prep for the SATs."

"Come spend the summer with us in Richmond. I will put you in summer school, and you will take SAT courses. Also, you will come to work in our factory. I think it will be a good experience for you to get out."

My parents and my uncle decided that I would matriculate in the summer program of the prestigious private school that my cousins Anjali, Shreya, and Neil attended and also take an SAT preparation course. I was enrolled in a physics course, but I really didn't enjoy it at all. The idea upon initially matriculating in a physics course was so that I would be stronger when I took the course during the regular academic year. My uncle encouraged me to drop the course once he saw how miserable I was. They encouraged me to take up creative writing, as that was another course option available and something they saw potential in me to excel in.

I met some interesting people in the class, and some were very talented. In fact, some had dreams of becoming authors and writers for big TV and media personnel. I was able to make *two friends* in the class: Ellen and Helena. Both Ellen and Helena were students at preparatory school, and they were also entering junior year for the 1999-2000 academic year. We had a lot in common in that we all played tennis. Ellen and Helena played on the varsity team, and they were aiming to be offered a scholarship to play in a Division 1 league. Both Ellen and Helena were ambitious and hard-working. We bonded over the stories we read about and discussed in class. Ellen, Helena, and I shared a lot of viewpoints on the stories discussed. We all enjoyed writing our own stories.

I found reading and writing stories to be somewhat cathartic, and the plays and books I read my junior year especially became very cathartic, particularly *The Glass Menagerie* by Tennessee Williams and *Catcher in the Rye* by JD Salinger. I appreciated how the plays and books, respectively, poured heart and soul into emotions and experiences that shaped such emotions as loneliness.

Apart from being stellar in sports and academics, Ellen and Helena had a very busy social schedule. Every weekend, they had some event or another to attend. We only got together once over the summer to see a movie in the theater, *Wild Wild West*. It felt great to be hanging out with people and experiencing what friendships could look like. I enjoyed the time I spent with them and wished we could've hung out more.

Anjali was living in New Jersey and attending law school. Shreya and Neil had their own bustling social lives. Even though the internet back then was nowhere near what it is today, particularly with social media, chatting on AOL messenger and playing computer games was enough to occupy anybody, especially Neil.

As the summer progressed, I got to meet Shreya's best friend, Charlene, when she came over to see a movie with Shreya. Shreya was attending a pre-medical program at an acclaimed university in Richmond. My aunt and uncle were heavily encouraging Shreya to take me with her to the beach party she was attending with her friends from both college and high school. Shreya had major hesitation, and I could tell she was starting to feel uncomfortable with her parent's insistence. The major cue I picked up on was the hesitation she had in her voice, akin to what I have seen when a student gets called on and asked if they want to read out loud. In those cases, the student complied even if the desire wasn't really there.

She eventually came up with an answer saying, "I don't want to expose Sonia to something that she has never been exposed to before. My friends drink."

I just told her not to worry about it, as I could tell she wasn't willing or wanting to take me. I also could understand if she just wanted it to be her and her friends. I wasn't bitter about it or angry. The whole 'friends drinking' wouldn't have bothered me, as I understood it was none of my business. Needless to say, it's not like I never saw people drink before.

Jay used to tell me about how he would hang out with Shreya and her friends when he was living in Virginia. Shreya and Jay were closer in age, so that helped with bonding. Jay shared about the time he felt validated by her and her friends. He spoke of how Shreya thought people misunderstood him because he was rebellious for a very justified reason: he wanted to live his own life that wasn't prescribed to him by fitting 'Indian standards.'

I was happy Jay was able to gain that closeness and validation. I sometimes wished that I would've received the same from others, but especially females on the spectrum were an enigma to others. After all, the autism spectrum wasn't very well understood at all back then versus more being known about it today. At times, I have received blowback and harsh criticisms from certain cousins for my idiosyncrasies and being the way I was with food rigidity, sensitivity, perseverance, and certain mannerisms and behaviors. I sometimes used to wonder if some of my relatives were embarrassed to be around me, and I often had those thoughts ring in my head quite loudly at times.

Anjali and Shreya were very privy to my emotional and social issues. There was a point where I used to call Anjali and Shreya when I was in eighth grade to have a chit-chat, as I wanted to at least feel closer to cousins if I lacked a social life. The only way I would hear from them was if I made the call. It would take time before I felt Anjali and I had more of a connection to one another out of the siblings.

Even though Shreya and Neil would be off doing their own things, one beautiful thing that arose out of the situation was the opportunity to spend quality time with my aunt and uncle. We went out to dinner one evening before seeing the movie *Notting Hill*. During dinner, there was a very good conversation, and my uncle led the majority of it, with my aunt chiming in at times. It was that conversation alone that would help change the trajectory of my life.

"So, Sonia, have you thought about your future more? You are entering your junior year this fall," said Uncle.

"I have been thinking about college, and I can't wait to graduate high school."

"Have you any idea what you would like to study?" he asked.

"I thought about medicine initially. Perhaps, maybe psychology," I responded, "with my heart leaning more into psychology."

"I understand your inclination towards medicine. After all, you grew up very influenced by your parents. However, let's be realistic. In order to get into medical school, you need to have certain prerequisites completed, two of which are chemistry and physics."

"I am aware of that."

"How did you do in chemistry?" asked Uncle.

"I got a 'C' in the course. I struggled and even had a tutor to help me through."

"So, it seems like you struggled," said Uncle.

"Yes, very much so."

"You know, if you got that grade in college for pre-med, it wouldn't be accepted. Medical schools are very particular about how they accept candidates. Point being, that grades in science subjects such as chemistry and physics are a very big deal. We know this because of Shreya," he stated.

"I see she works very hard."

"She does. I also see a lot of potential in you, too. However, I don't think medicine is it. I think you will do better in perhaps psychology or a different area of study," said Aunty.

"What makes you say that?" I asked with great curiosity.

"You are a very intellectual person and a thinker. You have a very good-natured personality. I also remember us having conversations about what you went through and have been struggling with at school," Aunty added.

"I have been thinking about psychology for a while. I even remember telling Dr. Shah about that, and she was supportive."

"Perhaps you ought to start going more towards where your strengths lie instead of what you feel you *have* to or are expected to do," said Uncle.

That conversation sparked a flame in me, one I had probably had all along. I was finally going to have a new anchor point to look forward to: envisioning my future with a new purpose! I was going to make something of myself and leave shit town Forest Ridge behind, and I was determined to get into a good college with my heart set on the East Coast. I was also eternally grateful to my aunt and uncle for all they had done, even though it may not have shown at the time.

Chapter 13

THE COAT IS PURPLE

I was keen on staying stuck to the bigger picture ahead. I planned my first visit to colleges during the fall break. I went with my mom to Virginia for four days, and we rented a car to drive to the places. The fall foliage was picturesque during the drive. I got to tour some of the campuses, and I met with college counselors. For the first time, I felt ecstatic about something. I was excited for the future, and I had my heart set on one of the colleges while I was there.

Classes in my junior year were going considerably better than what they were in my sophomore year. For one thing, I was taking more classes I enjoyed instead of courses I just 'had to do.' I even did a bold thing for myself and dropped my physics course after one semester. I was afraid to tell my parents at first, but I overcame the fear and told them at dinner one evening. Sooner or later, they would've had to find out because they hired a tutor for me. My dad looked like he would become infuriated at first, but to my surprise, he acted calmly when I explained that I dropped it to take psychology.

I started developing inappropriate crushes while I was a junior, namely on certain male teachers at the school. To be clear, nothing ever happened between me and the teachers I crushed on. It was only in my head that I was crushing on them, not quite understanding the extent of how unhealthy it was. I started seeing a new therapist as my junior year went on. Some of my depression was the fact I was still feeling very lonely and faced the occasional taunting and teasing of my past from students. Another part of the depression was that I was crushing on people whom I would never have.

Dr. Lopez worked on the second floor of a hospital that was dedicated to outpatient treatment. Dr. Lopez made me feel safe during the first meeting, and I was caught up to speed rather quickly with everything that happened. Dr. Lopez had a cheerful demeanor, yet she was authentic to who she was. Dr. Lopez made it a point to set some boundaries. "If there is ever a time I inadvertently say something to you or get angry with you, please speak up and tell me how you *feel*. I will work through this with you. I don't want you to get so hurt that you end up lashing out and calling me a 'bitch' like how your previous therapist worked you up."

"Thank you for that," I replied.

Dr. Lopez did a hands-on exercise with me about perspective during the first session.

"Sonia, what color is my coat that you see on the chair over there?"

"Purple."

"Correct. But what if I were to tell you that you were wrong? The coat is not purple, but rather, a mint green. Would you believe something was wrong with you for not thinking the coat was purple?"

"No."

"How come?"

"Because the coat is purple and not mint green."

"So, with regards to others, particularly the classmates who stereotyped you and made up their minds to shun you, can you remember that this is about them and not you anymore?"

"I will try. It just gets so hard because I feel really lonely."

"Yes, but remember the coat is purple. It's about them seeing the coat as mint green. In other words, you are who you are today, but they continue to see the younger 'acting up' Sonia."

"I will try."

"We will work through this together. Let's just try to make the remainder of your high school years bearable so you can move on with your life."

"That sounds good."

Dr. Lopez and I worked through a lot of the built-up emotions that I had been hiding, namely resentment and anger. I didn't realize that I had those emotions in me. Dr. Lopez was very blunt in expressing how she felt about the pent-up anger I had and how unhelpful it was for my own good. She was right.

Dr. Lopez and I used to talk about self-care. She explained that I needed to make sure I enjoyed my own company, especially on weekends or when there were events that I felt I might be left out of. We worked on identifying things I could do, such as watching good movies, watching TV, reading a good book, going for a drive to the bookstore or to a store, etc. These are all good skills to have, knowing how to take care of yourself, especially in light of when you feel the most triggered.

Throughout my junior and senior years, Dr. Lopez and I discovered the deeper reasons I was developing unhealthy crushes on male teachers that were aiding loneliness and depression. "Sonia, a lot of times, when people have a crush on older men, it is because they are missing something at home," Dr. Lopez explained. "They are looking for something they missed in their own father. What do you think of that?"

"Now that you explain it like that, it makes sense."

"So, let me ask you this. I know this is a hard question, but what do you feel is missing in your own father?"

"I just wished he would understand me more and not make me go to these Indian gatherings where I don't feel I belong," I said in a saddened voice.

"What happens when you go to these Indian events?"

"I get left alone, just like at school. I sit alone at tables. I get left alone, just exactly how I get left alone at school. It's no different."

"I can understand how that can be very painful, especially considering you deal with this on a constant basis at school," said Dr. Lopez quite empathetically.

"Yes. I just wished my dad understood I am not shy, something I am often accused of. I get blamed for my situation quite a bit, then get yelled at about how I don't ever pick up the phone. I don't really have anybody to call. It's not like when I was in middle school and always trying to call people to try to win over friends."

"I see," said Dr. Lopez.

Dr. Lopez continued. "That must be a very painful memory for you."

"It is. I still get reminded of what happened in sixth grade. Just the other day, I was sitting in Study Hall. One girl, around a group of her friends, asked, 'Hey Sonia, remember when you jumped out of the car?'"

Of course, a whole group of her friends were laughing. Thankfully, there were a couple of guys who were nearby who were part of their friend group and told me to just ignore them. I think they saw my facial expressions, as I was starting to get embarrassed and possibly upset."

"That was nice of those guys to stand up for you, but it was really mean on that classmate's part to bring up your past and judge you. I am so sorry this happened to you," said Dr. Lopez.

"She isn't alone in bringing up my past. My past was brought up before. One guy asked me if I had a smile on my face when I jumped out of the car. People started laughing upon hearing it. People write me off, and I am not given a chance. This is what my family fails to see. All they care about is a 4-star school district. I am tired of it."

"I can see how that can be frustrating and painful for you to deal with at school," said Dr. Lopez. "I think it's so important that you learn to stand up for yourself when you are being picked on, but also when you are strongly encouraged to attend these Indian events that don't go well for you or serve you any purpose."

"I have tried to say 'no' before, but I would get yelled at and accused of not wanting to socialize. I also get told how it doesn't look nice if I don't attend things with them."

"I can sense the anger and frustration behind this," said Dr. Lopez. "How would you feel about a family meeting?"

"I would be open to it," I responded quite enthusiastically. I was holding onto hope that perhaps something could change from a family meeting, and I was excited at the prospect of being advocated for.

Even though nothing changed with the family meeting, I appreciated the effort. I also started letting go of some of the anger and resentment with Dr. Lopez's persistent redirection so that I could focus on a brighter future. Dr. Lopez took the time to explain how the anger worked against me because it made me more bitter and stuck in the 'why me?' mode. Dr. Lopez was right. I heeded her advice to just focus more on the future.

Dr. Lopez was persistent: "You will get on with your life once you graduate from Forest Ridge High School." The more I heeded her advice to focus on the future, the brighter the future started to appear.

FINISHING OUT STRONG

My academic senior year started and ended strong! Remember how I was placed in a modified special education program? Would you believe I worked my way up to take an *Honors Spanish IV-level course and an AP Psychology* course? Can you believe I passed the AP Psychology exam to earn me credit for an Intro to Psychology college-level course?

Apart from becoming academically stronger, I started to become stronger mentally. I asserted myself by quitting the tennis team my senior year, as I felt tennis wasn't serving a purpose for me anymore. I was barely playing because seniors weren't allowed to play on JV, and I would have rather spent time continuing to be productive in academics. One of the main motivations for me to also quit was how people behaved when the tennis team went to an away meet, and we had to spend Friday night in a town outside of Indianapolis.

My parents drove down to watch the meet. They were asked to drive some of the girls to another area of town where there were more tennis courts. I was playing in the exhibition division, meaning it was more of a 'you're just here for fun' kind of deal. The team we were up against all played like professional tennis players, even the exhibition division. Safe to say, I ended up losing the game. Our school lost in the meet.

On the way to the place, the teammates whom we were transporting sat in the backseat, and I was sitting up front. They were whispering and laughing amongst themselves the whole time. One of the girls, Thalia, was one of the team's 'sweethearts' and was able to win everybody's approval. She was among the people laughing up a storm in the back with the girls and encouraging the others to laugh. They were being secretive and were whispering things they were laughing at.

When I tried to ask the girls what was funny, Thalia said, "Nothing," and she went on to whisper something else, treating us as if we were some random driver they hired to give them a ride.

My mom commented to me after the meeting about how disrespectful she thought the girls were. That was when I decided I no longer wanted to be part of a team where my parents were treated with that much disrespect after they had done the team a favor. I felt proud of myself and happy for standing up for myself and not continuing to be around additional disrespect.

My parents weren't upset about me quitting the team. My parents threw me a graduation party in that same time frame during the summer of 2001 as the ones I was coerced to attend by the Indian American Physicians Group. I was disregarded by my fellow classmates whose graduation parties I was obligated to attend and sat at tables alone. Of course, the graduates were giving tear-dropping speeches for all their friends, whom they made known during their speeches, and how they would be missed. I swear, I would've had a better time watching the Oscars for such tear-dropping speech moments. That was when the Oscars were still good, and the vast majority of movies were worth paying to see when they came out in theaters.

I would be filled with joy when it was time to leave such dreadful parties. I was excited about my own graduation party, though; it was the only one worth attending. I was quite surprised by the vast number of people who showed up. We didn't have any of those snobs from the Indian American Physicians Group, and thank God! Instead, my parents invited a different group of family friends. My extended family attended, too.

My aunt from Virginia was the emcee that evening, and she and other relatives gave lovely speeches about how proud they were of me. My aunt spoke of how I came to Virginia many times and how she grew to love me very much over the years, even more so that summer of 1999. I felt so touched by all the love, and for the first time, I lit up from inside. I was proud of myself and of what was the biggest victory of surviving all those years of Hell at Forest Ridge and getting accepted into college.

In fact, at my case conference meeting my senior year, it was hilarious watching the school administrators who were so quick to want to throw me out in sixth grade, stumble to find words about my college acceptance, high honor roll status, and an overall going out with a big bang on an academic level! *The coat is purple. Even though I made immense progress, people still were stuck in middle school acting out Sonia, the Sonia who wouldn't make it to eighth grade. Seven full academic years have gone by at this point, but yet they were still stuck in 1994. Now, it was my turn to say the words to Forest Ridge School District that they desperately wanted to say to me in 1994: Buh Bye!*

Chapter 14

THE ROAD TO DIAGNOSIS

HELLO, I THINK I KNOW HOW SONIA CAN BE HELPED

Mrs. Goldstein called my mom one day during the summer of 2001. A boy named Daniel, who was on the autism spectrum, was enrolling in my former elementary school. He showed some of the same symptoms that Mrs. Goldstein remembered that I had displayed in her fourth-grade homeroom class, including difficulty socializing, navigating social cues, and trouble with loud sounds. He needed a lot of guidance in understanding the social world and navigating his daily routine, such as getting on the school bus each morning. Because he was a person who was in need of more support, Daniel needed assistance with speech.

Because Daniel would be enrolling in Mrs. Goldstein's homeroom, she became thoroughly educated on the autism spectrum. As she learned more and more, her mind automatically raced to me. She called the house and immediately told my mom, "I think I know a way Sonia can be helped."

Mrs. Goldstein talked to Daniel's family and got permission for my mom and me to attend the meeting organized by the school to help Daniel acclimate to the upcoming school year. The meeting was in Daniel's backyard, which was large enough to host a considerable number of people. My former third-grade teacher was there, as well as other school staff, Daniel's classmates, and his relatives. A few college students were also in attendance, but they were studying in the respective fields where they would come into contact with those on the autism spectrum. The meeting had two autism specialists who helped lead and give guidance to suggestions that were beneficial for Daniel.

After the meeting, Mrs. Goldstein introduced my mom and me to the autism specialists, and they suggested that we continue our discussion. Since their offices were located near one of the major universities in Southern Indiana, they stayed at a nearby hotel. We met them there and started talking about my past history with sensory issues, the trip to Canada for hearing desensitization when I was in third grade, and the social issues and challenges.

Both ladies said that a lot of it reminded them of Daniel. They suggested that I might be on the spectrum. This started to pique my interest in autism to see if perhaps the diagnosis would finally be able to give an explanation as to why things were the way they were thus far.

FRESHMAN YEAR OF COLLEGE AND DR. LOPEZ'S GROWING CONCERN

I enrolled in a local branch of Tippecanoe University one week after matriculating in a private school elsewhere. I got too overwhelmed with all the change and had a complete meltdown. My parents thought it best to enroll me at a community college and then transfer me to the main campus so that I could go through the process at a slower pace. I first started out as a psychology major. I thought I would enjoy it, and there were certain courses that I did enjoy. However, when it came time to formally declare a major, my parents pressured me out of it and thought it better for me to study pre-law. They wanted more than anything for me to go to law school. I sometimes think it was my father's dream to be a lawyer…he would've been very good at it.

I saw Dr. Lopez upon the switching of schools. She would notice how I used to stick to certain interests, such as the crush I couldn't shake off of a teacher I had in high school when I was a senior. She used to notice certain behaviors, such as trying too hard with people at school and not making connections. In fact, freshman year of college was very lonely, and in many ways, it was like high school. The only difference was that I was around people who didn't know the 'acting out Sonia.' Instead, people already had friends from their respective schools, and some had families of their own, so they weren't looking to make new friends. I thought I was successful at making a friend out of English class, but that fizzled away rather quickly after we all hung out one weekend to catch a movie. Perhaps I gave off weird social cues that I wasn't aware of. I never got to find out what happened.

I used to work every Friday at my parents' clinic, as I didn't have class that day. That used to help break the routine. My parents had me join the tennis club to play with the high school group on Wednesday nights as a way to give me something to do. Dr. Lopez started bringing up getting neuropsychologically evaluated based on my continuing social difficulties and peculiarities with social skills.

Finally, towards the end of my freshman year of college, I took that set of examinations with a psychologist whom Dr. Lopez referred me to. The tests showed that I don't see things the way other people do, which causes me trouble when making friends. When the psychologist read the report, he suspected there was more to the story that went beyond a nonverbal learning disability. He referred me for further follow-up by a neuropsychologist whom he was well-connected with. The neuropsychologist appointment eventually happened at the start of the Fall 2002 Semester. I had other events come up before I was able to attend my appointment.

WELCOME TO SUMMER SCHOOL 2002

My cousin had a lot of his friends from college and work fly in for his wedding. I was inspired by the connections he had made throughout the years. I mean, for goodness sake, they flew across the world to attend his wedding! I was observant of how people connected to one another. As I had seen before, people were able to connect to others in a natural way. They were all quite a bit older than me, but when I reflect back on how I was at my age, I realize I wasn't very mature at all.

I was behind, and my cousin even thought I was much younger than my age because perhaps of some social cues I emitted and how I came across to people. I wasn't like the other girls at the wedding in that I didn't level up. Deep down, I knew I had a lot of growing to do in terms of presentation, self-care, social skills, etiquette, etc.

Nonetheless, I looked up to my cousin's friends and kept them in mind when I started the semester of 2002 at Tippecanoe University's main campus. I looked to them as examples of whom I would've liked to have been. I didn't know who I was nor what kind of girl I was in the way I do today. My roommate, Janet, was already settled into the room by the time my parents and I came to the Chancellor Hall. Chancellor Hall was a graduate dorm, but students who were aged 20 and up could live in that dorm during the regular academic year.

Janet was 20 years old when we met. She appeared a lot more mature for her age, and the way she spoke about the world suggested that she had a lot of life to her beyond her age. Janet gave a good first impression and appeared bubbly and very cheerful. She had a smile that could light up a room, and I would come to see over the semester that her sense of humor was such that she could've easily been a stand-up comedian.

I got to learn more about Janet when we went for a walk on campus that evening. Being the small world that it can be at times, I discovered that Janet grew up in a town about 20 minutes away from Forest Ridge called Jackson Heights. Jackson Heights used to be a booming town and place to eat and shop during the 1980s when the steel mills and automobile factories were at a peak. It was like a city away from Chicago.

However, due to the economic hardships that such industries fell victim to, the place unfortunately was left destitute and not ideal for families to live in. Janet told me about her family, which was quite a large family with many siblings. Janet had a passion for cooking, and she described herself as an incredible cook whose family enjoyed her scrumptious food. We ended up having a rather intellectual conversation as the walk went on. We must have walked at least five miles that evening.

Janet went on about how her father served in the US military for some time, and he would tell Janet and her siblings stories about the military. She described her father as being very diligent and stern yet very loving and affectionate towards his family.

Janet described her mother as affectionate and loving but quite direct with others. "If my mother has an opinion about folks, she lets them know. She doesn't beat around the bush," said Janet emphatically.

It would take some time before I saw how Janet was much like her mother. Janet wouldn't deny she was her mother's daughter after all.

She told me about how her mother and father met for the first time, a story that very much resonated with that of a movie scene. They met in an elevator at their mutual friend's apartment, and it became love at first sight.

Janet spoke highly of the life lessons her parents offered her and what she learned from listening to their lived experiences. In the course of the discussion, Janet shared a major life lesson that she and her parents learned: "The best revenge you could ever take on anybody in life is *to just live your life.*" This was something I had already known all too well by then.

IT'S NICE TO MEET YOU

When classes started, the Resident Assistant had a meet and greet for the girls who were living on the floor. The people who were in summer school were either going to be sophomores like me or were juniors and seniors. A lot of people who lived on the floor were only there during the week, but they used to leave during the weekends to either visit boyfriends back in their respective hometowns or visit friends who were back home for the summer. I had a chance to at least get to know a few other floormates, even if we didn't get to hang out too much outside of floor activities.

It wasn't long before I noticed a handsome Indian guy working at the Chancellor Hall front desk. I remember first seeing him when I was checking into the dorm. His name was Sameer. I thought he was incredibly cute. It was not long before I started developing a crush on him. What got me hooked on him was simple: he paid me some attention and was really nice to me. A cute guy being nice to me was not something I really ever had.

One time, while he was working at the desk, he asked me about how I was doing, food-wise, because the dorm's cafeteria, called the Retro Metro, was closed for construction that summer. We started talking a little bit. As we conversed, I noticed there were two girls sitting nearby who were keenly listening in on our conversation. I had seen one of the girls around him before, but I was not quite sure if they were boyfriend and girlfriend. I hoped they would chime in the conversation, but they were more interested in watching.

I ended up meeting the girl, Alisha, at a game night organized for Chancellor Hall by the Resident Assistants. We played a card game together, and she enjoyed the quirky jokes I was able to throw out there. I am sure many of you have picked up on it by now.

During the summer of 2002, I took two courses: social psychology and Spanish. My social psychology course was a start in understanding human behavior, something I had been interested in for many years despite all the social difficulties. Even though it didn't teach how to make friends, it taught about how people act toward others, especially when it comes to getting something they want from others. The material in the class was easy to learn; however, applying it to daily life took time to figure out. Making a friend in that social psychology class helped. Kareena happened to approach me after class to ask me my name and introduce herself. She was also of Indian descent, so she made connections that way by trying to find commonalities in our respective cultural heritage.

Kareena was just a very positive person with a lot of upbeat energy. She was quick to accept me with open arms, and she even introduced me to a couple of her friends who would join us sporadically when we would eat lunch together. Kareena and I used to eat lunch after class at the Student Union Cafeteria, which was located right at the center of campus. The Union was a 'go to' place for many events such as cultural events, salsa nights, and fraternity and sorority galas and functions.

Apart from the Union having elegant ballrooms, it also had computer labs, spacious seating areas for people to study, and a TV room that very much resembled an elegant living room.

Kareena was graduating that August of 2002. She was one of those people who would leave campus on weekends to visit her grandparents in Ohio. Kareena's grandfather was recovering from a stroke.

As we got to know each other more, I shared about Sameer: "You know, there is this really cute Resident Assistant, Sameer, in Chancellor Hall."

"Wait, I think I know Sameer. Is his last name Gandhi?"

"Yes."

"Oh, yes, I do know him. He already has a girlfriend, though. I think her name is Alisha."

"Oh, okay. I am happy for them. Kinda sucks I set my sights on someone who was taken," I said with disappointment and embarrassment.

"Oh Sonia, I completely understand. It happens. It happened to me before, too."

As Alisha and I got to know each other better, I asked her, "Are you and Sameer in a dating relationship? If so, how long have you been seeing each other?"

"We're just friends," was her reply.

The stories I heard from others about how Alisha and Sameer acted when around each other didn't add up. Janet told me she saw them holding hands when they were walking around campus. My Resident Assistant told me the same thing about Sameer and Alisha dating.

I didn't understand, at the time, why someone would feel the need to lie about being in a relationship. Knowing what I know now, Alisha's untruthfulness about being in a relationship was a major indicator that her and Sameer's relationship wasn't all that.

Some of the repeat behaviors I have done in the past were replicated yet again in terms of not being able to let go of a crush easily. I got super excited about the prospect of a new crush, and I acted like the little girl all over again who went and told everyone. Some floormates of mine knew about it, my Resident Assistant knew about it, Janet knew about it, Kareena knew about it, and even people from my Spanish class knew about it. I might as well have announced it in the college newspaper at the rate I was going. That way, all students on campus could've been let in on it! And wouldn't it have been an epic way to find out someone likes you? This was urban legend material right here! You know I'm not wrong on this!

DEALING WITH DRAMA AND NEGATIVE FEEDBACK

Things started out smoothly at first with Janet in that we were both busy with our respective classes. I would attend classes and go to the gym, and I would spend a lot of time studying during the week. Janet and I used to hang out during the weekends at The Village. The Village was basically an area down the street from campus that was sectioned off and shaped like a square. The Village was predominantly bars and fast food restaurants where people could go eat after the bars closed.

Outside the bar areas were tables, which came in handy for sitting outside and people-watching. Each bar at the Village had its own charm and attracted different kinds of people. People who enjoyed dancing would go to The Tap, where there was a dance floor towards the back of the bar. Next to the Tap was Tippecanoe Sports Bar. Across the street was another bar called Pool and Darts Bar. Apart from the pool and darts, the bar had a huge seating area for people to just sit, drink, and chill.

A little further down from campus, within walking distance, was a dance club called Beats that had Thursday specials of mixed drinks. There was Joe's Piano Bar two doors down from the dance club, where they played classics, and it was a great sing-along environment. Janet taught me a lot about alcohol and the kinds of drinks out there. I tried champagne once before in a family setting when I was 13. I never drank apart from trying the champagne one time at that point. People who were out and about put on quite a show at times, which was quite comical.

As much as I appreciated what I learned from Janet, I didn't always appreciate her tone of voice. There were times when I felt her tone was quite condescending, and I would get defensive. Janet used to make remarks like, "You always have something to say back, don't you?"

One incident stood out where we had a full-out blow-up. It was in the evening, and Janet had just come back to the room from working out.

"Sonia, you won't believe who I saw at the gym today! It's no one that you know."

Trying to be funny, I said jokingly, "Sameer?

"Didn't I just say it's no one you know? Didn't I just say that!?" She was practically screaming at me.

"Calm down!" I said.

"You know what, I am not even going to bother telling you the story."

Later on, we spoke again.

"Sonia, you really upset me."

"Janet, I didn't really like the way you treated me earlier today. You were yelling at me, and I don't think that was fair."

"I wasn't yelling at you."

"Well, that's what it felt like to me."

"Sonia, that's just how I talk. I'm boisterous. I have a big voice. It's no big deal."

"It was to me."

"You really do take a lot of stuff personally. You really do."

"So?" I said, taken aback. I was at a loss for words.

"So, what you should be saying is that *you* are sorry, and you will try not to do that anymore. *That's* what you are supposed to be saying!"

She left the room to go shower. I was upset and in tears at that point. I felt horrible about myself because her tone of voice reminded me of all the years I had been treated poorly and subsequently made to feel poorly.

I went for a walk to self-soothe. I used to like to go to the middle of campus where the bell tower and Tippecanoe fountain were located. There were benches where people were able to sit near the fountain. The cool thing about the fountain was that it looked like a candle flame when it was lit up. As you got close, you could see the different colors of the rainbow light up on the sides of the fountain. I used those sensory objects—the Bell Tower and the Tippecanoe Fountain to help myself calm down. Not just that night but in general. I used those sensory objects to help me reflect and contemplate my future.

Janet and I made up later in the evening. She understood where I came from, or so I thought. I kind of got the sense I had to be careful around Janet, and I started feeling that I had to walk on eggshells around her because I never knew what kind of Janet I would get.

In the meantime, I also started becoming weary of Janet's friend, Janelle, who also lived on our floor. There were certain things that I found off-putting. She would always come to the room and ask for food, and she helped herself to the room as if it were a room in her own house. Janelle would be sitting talking to Janet on her side of the room, and there were times when I would listen to music. Janet didn't mind the music as much, and we used to bond over some music, but Janelle would ask me to turn *my* music down. I didn't want to start drama, especially since I was somewhat distrusting of Janet's temperament, so I acquiesced.

There were times I would try to hang out with Janelle and Janet when they were hanging out in Janelle's room as an effort to bond and connect. I would act like Janelle would act by knocking on the door and coming in, but she didn't like that.

Janelle used to say, "I didn't ask you to come in."

Even though I was trying to mirror behavior, there was a lot to be learned from the blowback.

What was most shocking was how I came home after my Spanish class one afternoon to find Janelle asleep in *my bed*. I guess Janet and Janelle were hanging out in the room, and instead of considering how I might want to rest after class, boundaries were crossed big time by how Janelle fell asleep in my bed. Janelle's actions went beyond human decency and respect for another person. What was worse was that Janelle used to have pungent body odor, which I believe was unfortunately attributed to her health condition. After I requested Janet that Janelle not sleep in my bed, it never happened again.

I was unaware of how I came across socially the majority of the time, even though deep down, I may have felt something wasn't right. I just didn't know what exactly to identify.

"Listen, Sonia," Janet said, "Janelle and I think we should talk."

"Ok," I said. "What do you want to talk about?"

"Look," Janelle said, "we know you like Sameer a lot, but the thing is.... The thing is,"

Janet butted in, "Is that it's a little strange how you keep going on and on about him. He's unavailable. He has a girlfriend. You and him, it's not gonna happen."

"She's right, you know," Janelle said. "Sometimes you just have to forget it and move on. Do you know what I mean?"

"Kinda," I said.

"I just don't get it," Janet said. "It's just kinda weird that even though you know this guy is seeing someone, you keep telling everyone you meet about Sameer and how you like him. Ya know, people just don't do that."

Janelle added, "Sonia, sometimes it's good to keep some thoughts and feelings to yourself, especially when they have no chance of going anywhere. I mean, do you really think it's fair to go on and on about him when he's got a girlfriend?"

"I hadn't realized I was doing that." In reality, this wouldn't have been the first time.

Janet continued, "Another thing, I think you get down on yourself when you compare yourself to Alisha. I know the whole 'what does she have that I don't?' runs through your head a lot."

"Maybe," I replied.

I never remembered feeling that way the times I hung around with Alisha. She and I ended up becoming friends throughout the summer, and there were moments when we hung out together.

"Even if Sameer was single, do you think he would get with you anyway?" Janet asked. "Look at you, and look at Alisha. Alisha is all bubbly. You're not."

This made me feel compared and brought back memories of how Dr. Shah used to compare me to other classmates, namely Zara.

"The difference between you and her is…" was a phrase I heard most often when I went to hell, I mean therapy with Dr. Shah. Most often, she praised the other person and put me down.

Janet said, "However, that doesn't mean you won't be a perfect match for someone else. Just take what you have and work with that."

Even though what Janet and Janelle said had some truth and merit to it, there is a way to address things. Comparing someone is a lot like shaming someone. If someone is already feeling down about themselves, comparing only makes them feel worse. I didn't have the skills back then to say, "You can't compare me to Alisha because she is who she is, and I am who I am."

My personality was just emerging at that time. Today, I have a bubbly, eccentric, quirky kind of personality, depending on the energy I pick up around others. Back then, I was just starting to come out of my shell, so people did not get to see who I really was. Truth is, I didn't even know who I was.

I was always intrigued by people who could have all the friends and were able to date. But I thought I was making progress because I had my friend Kareena from social psychology class to sit with and eat lunch every day. I also thought I was making progress because I was talking to more people, unlike how it was when I was younger.

I expressed to Janet and Janelle that I was doing a good enough job being social and making friends, but without even saying the words, Janet made a face that even I could read.

"No, you didn't."

The negative feedback didn't end with Janet and Janelle. A floormate, with whom Janet and Janelle connected well, invited me to go bowling with her during finals week after quite a few people had left, including Janet, to go home for the break. I was getting picked up after my Spanish final the next day.

The floormate tried to strike up a conversation in the bowling alley that was located on the basement level of the Union. She was quick to notice things that were lacking, such as a lack of experience with bowling. I may have gone bowling when I was very young, but it was not something that became regular. The floormate was somehow able to pick up on a lack of socialization.

"So, Sonia, let me ask you. What have you been doing for the past few years? Living under a rock?"

"Why would you ask that?" I asked, astounded.

"It seems like you really don't have much experience with things," the floormate said, somewhat puzzled.

"I am just getting in the process of socializing," I responded.

"Yeah, it seems like making and keeping friends has been a problem for you," she said unabashedly.

"I am working on it," I said. "I didn't have friends growing up and was ostracized. It's a rather long story that I would rather not get into."

"It seems like you don't make friends easily, unlike Janet and Janelle," said the floormate.

"I am working on friendships. Why don't you think I made friends this summer?" I asked out of curiosity, and to see whether she thought along the same lines as Janet and Janelle.

"Well…it's just that, it's just that compared to Janet and Janelle, it seemed like they made more friendships," the floormate said.

There were times when I used to notice the floormate sitting with Janet and Janelle in my room. I noticed the difference in the energy Janet and Janelle had when they were with the floormate versus how they were around me. The smiles and happiness weren't quite the same. These were social cues missed at the time that would've been a giveaway that perhaps something was disingenuous. I wouldn't be surprised if Janet and Janelle talked about me to that floormate, which probably encouraged her to ask the kinds of questions she asked so boldly without even knowing me well.

Even though I may not have been as quick to pick up on the social cues, I was observant of energy. I was also observant of how I was treated in comparison to other peers. Overall, all the feedback from people fueled my inclination to get an appointment with the neuropsychologist.

Chapter 15

WELCOME TO YOUR DIAGNOSIS

AT LAST!!

Right at the beginning of the Fall 2002 Semester, I made an appointment to see the neuropsychologist. She reviewed the results of the psychological exam, reviewed my past history up to that point, and I filled her in on all the feedback I received from the summer. She then went ahead and asked me some questions.

"Sonia, how do you think your behavior came off this past summer?"

"That I didn't live up."

"Do you think it is typical for people your age?" she asked.

"No," I said.

She continued, "That behavior is very much like a child."

"Oh," I said, feeling embarrassed.

"Sonia, one thing I should tell you is that you are more at risk of being taken advantage of and used."

"How so?" I wondered.

"You are a bit naive, as shown by the tests. You also are immature for your age, which sets you up big time," said the neuropsychologist.

"Oh," I responded, feeling sad.

"I strongly urge you to think twice before you even think of picking up a drink. I am sure you know by now that Tippecanoe University has quite a party scene," said the neuropsychologist.

"Yes, I am aware of it," I said.

"Just remember one thing; you could easily be made to laugh and be the one made to dance on a table while everyone enjoys fun at your expense," she said sternly.

"I will remember," I responded.

My mother attended the session with me. The neuropsychologist did a complete and thorough breakdown of the psychological exam. The exam showed developmental delay alongside autistic traits. She said the magic words, "Sonia has Asperger's Syndrome," which is now considered the autism spectrum disorder.

The appointment left me with a huge bag of mixed emotions. On the one hand, I was thrilled that I finally got the blindfold taken off and could see the maze with clear eyes. There was a lot that depression didn't explain in terms of difficulties, sensory issues, and social issues. However, there was a part of me that felt a bit like, "Why couldn't I have been born normal? Why does it have to all be so difficult? Why did I have to live in a world where people don't understand?"

It was all so freeing, yet so painful simultaneously.

Chapter 16

THE MAZE POST-DIAGNOSIS

DR. THEROUX AND NAVIGATING FAKE FRIENDS

At the end of the Summer Semester, I had to move all of my things out of the dorm room because only people aged 20 and up could live in that building. My birthday was the first week of the Fall 2002 Semester, but it wasn't enough to allow me to stay at that dorm. I moved into a dorm further away from campus, and that dormitory was filled with a lot of freshmen and a good number of sophomores.

I got invited by two floormates when I first moved into the dorm to go to a concert thrown at the Lawn that evening. I didn't know about the band, but I learned that they were brought to campus and sponsored by the Christian Co-Op group on campus. The band was playing secular pop hits. I wanted to go to the Village to watch people, like I used to do over the summer once the concert ended. I didn't realize how conservative the girls were whom I walked to the concert with until they told me their reason for not wanting to go. "There are too many drunk men there, and that goes against what we stand for," said the girls.

When we got back to the dorm, my new roommate, Wendy, was already in the room. Wendy was on the phone when I got back, and she looked excited to meet me. Wendy was from southern Texas, and she had a bit of that southern Texan accent. She grew up in a conservative household, and she had impeccable manners.

Wendy was studying management, and she was a studious person. She had a small group of friends, and she had a good aura about her. I felt comfortable around her right away. Wendy could tell I was nervous about starting my sophomore year. We spoke about what to expect when I see a full campus of 40,0000 students.

"Sonia, it may seem overwhelming at first, but just keep focused," said Wendy. "Go to your classes, and you will meet people in your major, just like how you met people this summer. The only difference is the classes will be fuller."

"Thank you for letting me know this and helping reassure me that everything is going to be okay, Wendy."

"You are so welcome! You've got this!" she encouraged.

Even though my anxiety was sky-high, I managed to get through my first official day with a full campus late in August 2002. It took some getting used to being around such a vast student population and not seeing people I was used to seeing over the summer—a good thing for the phone directories we had on campus. Cell phones weren't what they are now. Texting wasn't really a thing back in 2002, either, and cell phone calls were only free after 9:00 p.m. The rooms all had phones, and there was a way you could dial another person as long as they lived on campus.

I called Janet at the start of the semester. She had moved to a dorm a little further away from where I was staying. She had gotten a part-time job in addition to taking courses. We planned to try to meet at some point.

Before Kareena graduated, she referred me to a therapist who worked on campus and taught abnormal psychology. I wanted to get support right away, especially since I was just diagnosed with Autism Spectrum Disorder. I was having a hard time moving past what happened over the Summer 2002 Semester with all the negative feedback and falling for someone unavailable. I was very anxious about all the changes and navigating the maze socially now that I was able to have a vision of it.

I had an initial phone conversation with Dr. Theroux. She sounded so sweet and had a soft tone of voice. There was something about the way she kept saying my name that just felt so comforting. One thing I appreciated about Dr. Theroux was her honesty.

"Sonia, I should be honest with you and let you know that you are the first person that I am working with who has Asperger's Syndrome. However, the things you told me over our brief phone conversation are still areas I could help with as far as friendships and dealing with rejection are concerned."

Her honesty and confidence in what her abilities were what enticed me to book a session with her.

Dr. Theroux used to ask me about how I interacted with people. "Sonia, when you meet someone new, what do you talk about? What do you say or ask to get a conversation started?"

"Well, I talk to people about parties because I know parties are a popular topic for many college students."

"What do you say about them?"

"I'll ask people if they've been to any interesting parties lately."

"Then what happens?"

"Sometimes they say 'yes,' but then they might not say anything else."

"Like, what?"

"Like other conversation starters? I might ask them about their favorite drink."

"Do you drink?"

"No. I'm only 20, and I don't have a fake I.D."

"And does asking about their favorite drink get the conversation going?"

"Sometimes."

Perhaps some conversation starters could've been addressed and more role plays conducted. Dr. Theroux used to reinforce the idea that other people had a lot of practice with socialization and had already learned how to make and keep friends.

She would say, "Just keep doing what you are doing to put yourself out there and talk to people."

Throughout the semester, I tried to become intentional about how I put myself out there. I spoke to Kareena over the phone, and she strongly encouraged me to attend a Bollywood movie night that she knew the Indian American Students Association put on at the beginning of the year. Oddly enough, I saw flyers for it around campus. I, therefore, attended the movie because I figured I had nothing to lose.

The movie was playing in a lecture hall in the Math and Engineering Hall. Of course, the Math and Engineering building was picked truly in brown fashion! The acoustics for displaying the movie weren't good. The sound kept echoing, which made watching the movie difficult. It wasn't long before the people kind of checked out and started having side conversations with their friends. Hey, where were the tech people amongst the brown people in attendance?

There wasn't a very big group of people who showed up. It was mainly one friend group who attended the event. She was one of the main organizers of the Bollywood movie night. I ended up having a conversation with one girl from that entire group. She shared with me a story about her parents and how they had a rough time getting married due to religious differences. She also moved to India from California when she was a teenager. She shared her experiences of the transition and how she learned to love her experience.

I only hung out with that group maybe two other times. The first time was to catch a movie at the theater. I missed the social cue, though, because the movie organizer was mainly into her boyfriend that whole time. They were holding hands, and her friends had to tell me indirectly to give them their space. A majority of the people in her group were cordial, and you could tell they had very tight connections within their group. I got to observe how that group interacted at times when I would eat dinner in the next dorm over, and they happened to be eating at the same time. They were discussing plans they had made for Friday evening, and they had it so that all the couples would hang out together. The movie organizer said it was a 'couples night only' event.

The other people in the group who weren't in a couple made plans to get together and do their own thing. I remember going back to my dorm after dinner and sharing what happened with my roommate, Wendy.

She thought having the 'couple's only night' was awful. I, too, felt something was off about that energy, but I wasn't quite sure what it was. In hindsight, the energy I felt was exclusionary and exclusiveness of the group.

The last time I hung out with that group was for the organizer's birthday. I had called and left her a voicemail. She returned the call by inviting me to her birthday celebration. I met some new people that night, and for the most part, the only people I ended up getting along with the most were the new people I met who were not of Indian descent. Can you all start to see a theme by now that how I interact at cultural events is like trying to mix oil and water?

I invested energy in getting to know other people from my classes. I had gotten better at conversation skills that I would have sporadically used with peers, and I was able to connect with one classmate outside of class. During my Foods and Nutrition course, people were assigned to take samples of different kinds of food from sample cups so that we could see how taste buds react to different types of food. A classmate, Amy, volunteered to get mine and another person's in the row.

I got to know Amy after that class. She and I hung out one weekend because she invited me to a party that her sorority house threw. Amy's sorority was nonsecular. Hence, even though there was a party, no alcohol was permitted. The music played was dance hits, but clean versions of the songs. Quite a number of people showed up, mainly people who really loved to dance. I didn't really have dancing skills like other people did at that party, and I got more amusement from watching others dance. Amy and her boyfriend drove me home a couple of hours after the party started; they had other plans to hang out for a while.

The only person I stayed in relatively constant contact with was Alisha, the girl from summer who was Sameer's girlfriend. Alisha and Sameer broke up at the start of the Fall Semester. I was shocked to find out such news, especially because when we all hung out in a group the last time, they looked very much in love. Alisha, her roommate, Sameer, and I were hanging out in the TV room. They all ordered a pizza, but I had already eaten a good dinner. I noticed how Alisha was practically hand-feeding Sameer a slice of pizza. I found it kind of corny but also kind of cute. I guess I was intrigued because I never saw a couple act in quite that way. The only ways I saw couples interact was through hand-holding, hugging, and kissing, which you normally would see.

Alisha and I used to get together once a week to grab dinner. I met a lot of people through Alisha while she continued living in Chancellor Hall. Alisha and I went to on-campus events together, such as the major Diwali show that drew in hundreds of people and was held in the campus auditorium. Our friendship grew so that we were able to have in-depth conversations about life, lived experiences, hopes, dreams, etc. Towards the mid-semester, Alisha mentioned that she had started dating someone new. He was a guy she knew from where she grew up, and they started dating not too long after she broke up with Sameer.

I had an opportunity to meet Alisha's boyfriend when he came to visit her one weekend. Similar to Sameer, he was really handsome but even better looking than Sameer. The question that started running through my mind was how it was that people could get over a relationship and start dating someone else right away.

College was the perfect time for people to experience dating and having a relationship. I was nowhere close to even knowing how to do that, let alone get comfortable enough to even have male friends. I didn't know how to talk to guys at large, and I used to get scared. A lot of my fear was that of being laughed at due to how guys treated me growing up. However, I wanted to experience what I saw other people have; hence, there lies the conundrum.

I was able to develop a deeper connection with Wendy over time, similar to how I developed a deeper connection with Alisha. Wendy and I also hung out sporadically. We used to go running together inside the gym on the top floor, where there was an indoor track. I enjoyed running. Wendy ran very fast, and she pushed the pace.

I kept in touch with Janet, but compared to Wendy, Alisha, and even Amy, I still felt I had to walk on eggshells around her. Case in point: When I shared with Janet how I went for a run with Wendy, she commented, "That doesn't strike me as something you would do."

I told her I liked the run. Janet didn't say much after that. With time, I would see how Janet had me in a box she created as to how she thought I was and how she thought I should be.

INNER HALL TRANSFER AND SHOCKING NEWS

Before the end of the Fall Semester, I applied for a transfer to Chancellor Hall because I wanted to be closer to campus, especially since winters get quite cold. I wanted to live in a quieter dorm. It got approved just before Thanksgiving.

Wendy was understanding when I told her I was moving back to Chancellor Hall. She was planning to move to an off-campus apartment as soon as the year ended. Wendy didn't like not having a kitchen and wanted to have more space. The next person I spoke with was Alisha.

"Hi, Alisha. It's Sonia."

"Hi, Sonia. What's up?"

"You're not going to believe this, but guess what?"

"What?"

"I got in! I'm moving back to Chancellor Hall."

"Oh Sonia, I'm so happy for you. I know that's what you've wanted."

"I guess we get to see each other even more now, huh?" (Laughs)

"Sonia, actually, I'm moving."

"Moving?"

"I'm going back to India."

"What?! Get out of here! When?"

"I'm taking my exams early—before Thanksgiving—and I won't be coming back."

I said bye to Alisha Sunday evening, going into the week of Thanksgiving break. I had exams that Tuesday before Thanksgiving break started on Wednesday. I shed tears when I said bye to Alisha. I was sad that I was losing a friend, but this time, I was losing a friend due to circumstances and not because of my own doing. A major part of my sadness was also driven by fear. I was afraid I wouldn't find another close friend I could see once a week. My fear and sadness were short-lived because the end of the semester was around the corner, which meant a lot of papers due and final exams.

During the week of finals, Janelle saw me walking on campus as I was heading to the computer lab to get my final paper for my criminology class printed. She pulled me aside, which surprised me as she had given me the cold shoulder at the start of the Fall Semester when I ran into her in one of the computer labs on campus and said, "Hey Sonia, I hear you're moving back to Chancellor."

"Yes, I am," I replied.

"You are going to be on my floor, the ninth floor. I know who your roommate is; her name is Tracy. Actually, you are going to be two doors down from me."

"I got notified of my room assignment and of my roommate. Is she nice?"

"Tracy is very kind. She is, like you, very intelligent and studious. We get along quite well."

"Oh great!"

"But, there is something I wanted to discuss with you that I think is very important for you to know. There is a lot of drama on the ninth floor, Janelle said."

"What kind of drama?" I questioned.

"There are people who will be nice to you in front of your face but stab you in the back. Knowing how you are, I know that you tend to be naive. I am just asking you to please be careful about whom you trust and share things with. Not everybody is out to be your friend. Just remember what we told you at the end of summer about keeping certain things to yourself," said Janelle.

"Thank you for letting me know," I said gratuitously.

I heard from others, namely Alisha and Janet, that there was drama on the ninth floor before this conversation. Janet used to go visit Janelle during the fall, and she shared stories with me about what she observed. Alisha used to comment about how the Resident Assistant, Nadia, complained all the time about drama on her floor.

NOT READING PEOPLE RIGHT, AND SOCIAL BLINDNESS

Winter break lasted a full month. I got to relax and spend time at home. It felt odd not having anything to do as far as attending classes, studying, and going to the gym. I spent time with my parents. I tried reaching out to Alisha to see how she was doing, but I hadn't heard back from her. Janet's birthday fell over the holidays. In fact, she and I celebrated her birthday together. We went out to lunch and to a bookstore after. Janet came over to hang out at my house, and my parents surprised her with a gift stationery set. She was appreciative, but I didn't realize how much she harbored resentment towards me until the start of the Winter Semester.

I moved into Chancellor Hall the Saturday before the start of the Winter Semester 2003. My roommate, Tracy, was still at home. I saw that she had a lot of pictures and a poster of sorority events hung up on her side of the room. I finally got to meet her the next day. Tracy had a lot of friends, and she was on her cell phone a lot throughout the day. We went to a supermarket together because she forgot some things she needed.

After winter break, I was in the computer lab finishing a homework assignment. One of Alisha's friends, Sapna, whom I met briefly, happened to also be in the computer lab. I had reached out to Alisha a couple of times to just say hello and try to keep in touch. Sapna happened to catch Alisha on messenger and said, "Sonia, guess who is online? Alisha!"

"What?! I remember reaching out to her and not hearing much back from her."

"Sonia, I will go ahead and let her know to hit you up as soon as possible."

I was sensitive, and my mind went into rejection mode right away. Unlike today, where I am able to give people more of a benefit of the doubt and perhaps look past it, back then, it was automatically a dichotomous 'all or nothing' way of thinking. This is common for many people on the autism spectrum to have an 'all or nothing' way of thinking due to how their brains process information. My basis was that I hadn't heard from her, and I was informed she was talking to others online.

I felt depressed and left a voicemail for Janet so I could get some perspective. Not only was Janet quick to jump on the chance, she was quick to knock me down after I had already been down. She started out kindly before dropping the ball.

"Sonia, I am so sorry to hear that Alisha did that to you. You don't deserve to be treated that way. I have been noticing this for a while, and I am just going to go ahead and tell you what I see: the problem with you is that you only like pretty people with long black hair as your friends. Alisha was beautiful, thin, and *everything you wanted to be*. That's why you wanted her to be your friend, and you did everything you could to make her your friend. But you don't consider *me* a friend, and I'm here for you, always. This is some shit. This is really some shit."

"Janet, I consider you my friend," I said, rather shocked.

"Well, that is good."

Even now, I feel so embarrassed to even be writing this because I should've told her to screw off.

Janet went on, practically screaming, "Another problem with you is you think everybody is your friend. That is on YOU! People who meet you are only acting out of common courtesy, something learned at home.

Not everybody who is nice to you is trying to be your friend. You have this image of a friend."

"I am learning how to make friends. I didn't have any friends. It would be nice to have a group of friends."

"Sonia, what sounds better to you? One friend whom you could trust or having a group where you don't even know if you could trust them?" Janet asked in a rather emphatic manner. "When I was in high school, I had a clique, a name, everything. Now, it is just me by myself," Janet continued.

I was thinking to myself, 'Gee, I wonder why?!'

"I guess the one friend," I answered.

"Exactly! You have an image of a friend! All you get are backstabbers and users."

This speaks volumes from someone who was that way herself. There were times Janet spent time with my family when my parents came to visit on a weekend, and she enjoyed a paid-for lunch. Janet enjoyed a paid-for birthday lunch. She enjoyed receiving birthday gifts, all for her to turn around and act like this.

Janet continued in her snarky attitude and tone, "Look, I don't like to beat around the bush. I am going to say things as is!"

"I know I am a nice person," I retorted.

"Are you genuinely nice?" she questioned.

At this point, I should've said, "Then why do you associate yourself with me if this is what you honestly think?"

This would've made her question herself and her own genuineness. If a person feels that they have to be 'friends' with someone out of moral obligation, or if a person feels that the other person owes them gratitude for being a 'friend,' that's not a genuine friendship.

What Janet did should've been a clue that perhaps it was time for this 'friendship' to end. That conversation was the perfect setup to leave a toxic friendship! Sadly, I hung onto this friendship until we had a falling out in the summer of 2003. A lot of this hanging on was reinforced by the fact that this is what I felt I deserved, especially having been told that I was unworthy of having a friend and people like me ruin the world. Also, the years of ostracism and alienation, being forced to go to events where I was not accepted and made to either sit on floors or tables alone, reinforced that I was unworthy and needed to be destroyed.

Dr. Theroux worked with me on my automatic 'all or nothing' way of thinking.

"Sonia, instead of jumping and believing the conclusions you made, why don't you first find out what is happening with Alisha? Maybe you should send her an email."

"I don't understand why she was chatting with Sapna online."

"Who reached out first?"

"I think maybe Sapna did. She saw her online and was the one that pointed it out."

"Okay, and so?"

"I thought Alisha didn't want to be my friend anymore because I hadn't heard from her after sending her emails."

"Hmm, does this automatically mean she doesn't want to be friends anymore, though? Let's explore other reasons."

"I don't know."

"Could it be possible that she just happened to be caught up with other things?"

"Could it be that perhaps she just happened to be on messenger because she was checking her emails? Could it be that she was trying to get in touch with a family member who was going through something? The possibilities are endless. We won't know until we first find out what has been going on with Alisha. I don't think it is fair to beat yourself up and jump to conclusions until you know the full story first."

"Okay, let me go ahead and send her an email."

Through the email process, I learned that Alisha's father underwent a major cardiac operation. I felt bad for how I reacted to the situation.

Janet didn't agree with the therapist, "Sonia, Alisha knew what she was doing."

"Alisha said her father underwent a major cardiac surgery."

"Then what is the mother there for? To sit and look pretty?! Bullshit!!" Janet exclaimed, exasperated.

The conversation with Janet made navigating the social world even that more challenging: Who was right? Time will tell.

The more I thought about Janet's behaviors toward me, the more I realized she never had anything positive to say about me.

If Janet complimented me, it would always come with a backhanded comment. For instance, Janet would tell me that I was very intelligent but would follow that with, "You shouldn't have to have other people tell you that."

I never asked. However, Janet had no reservations about anything negative, such as me not being confident enough, not this, not that.

Hence, this led me to a very important life lesson: Be careful whom you take advice from because not everyone has your best interest at heart.

Janet's inconsideration of Alisha's situation was her way of keeping control over me so she could continue to use me as a punching bag. This is a social cue that many people on the autism spectrum can miss; especially when they are navigating friendships, because they don't know what to look for in friendship material.

I should've ended the friendship with Janet when she gave me her attitude when I needed support. If anything, I learned this important lesson: Be mindful of whom you share your problems with and go to for advice. A person who is always putting you down and quick to point out the negative in you is not someone who has your back. Anybody can say they are your friend, and even though a real friend will keep it real with you, they don't always knock you down every chance possible.

There is a difference. A real friend will also see the greatness in you and celebrate what you have to offer instead of always finding faults.

Not Reading People Right

Naivete and trusting easily are not uncommon for people on the autism spectrum, particularly because they have trouble picking up on social cues and lack social experiences to know what to look for in people. However, with time and practice with social skills and socializing with others, they will become in tune with things to watch for and, more importantly, the energy they *feel* around others.

Apart from hanging out with Tracy when I first moved into Chancellor Hall, I connected with some floormates whom I thought were nice girls. We grabbed dinner together, and I shared what I thought were normal conversations about classes. They were discussing their dating lives with each other. I made the mistake of telling people I fell for someone who ended up not liking me back without sharing who. I may have been a little too excited when I first met people who seemed immature and off-putting. I was eventually told about this toward the end of the semester from another floormate. It wasn't long before I was made the story.

A floormate called me over when she saw me coming back to my room from the library one evening. She said, "Sonia, I think you should know that many girls are laughing at you right now. If you are having any issues, you should either come talk to me or the Resident Assistant, Nadia."

"Thank you. What exactly are people saying, though, and why?" I asked. I can honestly say I didn't remember what people would have to gossip about because I kept things at the surface level as much as possible. I heeded advice not to go into other people's rooms and kept mainly to myself as much as possible.

"I am not going to get into it, but you should know that this is going on. It's best you stay away from floormates at this time," warned the floormate.

"Okay, thanks."

I still hung out with some floormates when they would do group events, such as building game nights or when the girls from the floor organized a 'single girls' night out' during Valentine's Day.

The girls' night out consisted of dinner followed by going to the movie *How to Lose a Guy in 10 Days*. I wasn't aware that one of the floormates who organized these events and invited me, along with having brunch with me one time at a nearby Indian restaurant, was the same person who was telling people how repulsed she was by me. I came to find out later in the semester from Lucy herself.

I left feeling sensitive about it because I felt like no matter what I did, I was not making much progress. The Winter Semester of 2003 was quite lonely for the vast majority. I met with people sporadically throughout the Winter 2003 Semester. Apart from seeing Janet on occasion, I met with

Amy from the Foods and Nutrition class a couple of times. Amy ended up getting engaged to her boyfriend during winter break, and they were starting to plan their wedding.

I also connected with a friend, Estelle, from my Spanish class from the Summer 2002 Semester. I connected with a couple of people who lived in my building, one of whom I randomly met when I was visiting Alisha. I was just leaving, and Alisha was going to work at the front desk of Chancellor Hall. That was when Bianca was heading outside, and we ended up having a conversation as I was leaving. Bianca was part of the architectural program at Tippecanoe University, and that was not an easy program to get accepted into.

Bianca and I were similar in that we were always busy with classes and schoolwork. Bianca, because of the nature of her major, had to either visit sites or work on developing projects. We only saw each other a couple of times in the semester due to our schedules.

I randomly ran into Phaedra, with whom I had a class with in the Fall Semester. She and I sat near each other during class and had a couple of conversations about the material we were discussing in class. Phaedra and I got together a couple of times towards the end of the semester. The times happened randomly because we would happen to run into each other in the Chancellor Hall lobby. It was then Phaedra told me to stop by.

We just watched TV the first couple of times we hung out. Phaedra shared some of her experiences thus far at Tippecanoe University. I commented about how I noticed it could get lonely, surprisingly, on a campus of 40,000 people. That was when she shared how she used to be part of a big friend group earlier, but then she decided it wasn't worth being a part of anymore.

"I can see where you are coming from, Sonia. I used to be part of a big friend group when I first started college."

"If you don't mind me asking, when did you start at Tippecanoe?"

"I started here in 1999. I am set to graduate in December."

"Oh, cool," I said.

" I am excited to graduate. However, I wanted to address the point of loneliness you were making. I was part of a big friend group when I started college. However, it's not all what people think it is," said Phaedra.

"What happens in these groups?"

"Well, don't you remember high school and what it was like in social groups back there?"

"I, unfortunately, haven't had a lot of experience with that," I said, feeling somewhat ashamed. I further explained, "I am on the autism spectrum, so friendships never really came easy for me."

"Oh, okay. I understand now that you said that. I am going to fill you in on what happens in the groups: It's drama."

"Why all the drama?"

"Because people tend to get katty with one another. People will get mad at each other, talk poorly behind someone's back, and a lot of times there is jealousy and envy, especially around guys."

"Oh, I see," I said.

"If I can leave you with anything, please don't worry about not having that big friend group. Don't worry about not having someone to be around all the time because it is not all that," explained Phaedra.

"Thank you for sharing that!" Even despite the appreciation for what was said, the message didn't resonate right away.

Tracy was an observant roommate, and she was quite aware of the fact

I wasn't out as much as she was. There were times when she stayed in, but more often than not, she was with her friends at a sorority party or the next. She and I had a discussion about friendship-making.

Tracy said, "Part of making friends is knowing who you are and what you stand for. The reason I don't think people are coming and talking to you much is that they don't see the confidence in you and a person who knows who she is; whereas, people love to come to talk to me and others because we know who we are."

I felt compared yet again with the automatic thought that 'you don't live up like others.'

"I am working on it," I said.

"Yes, I think you are just learning how to make friends. I learned earlier how to make friends," Tracy said.

"Yeah, I am just learning," I said. "I never really had a lot of friends growing up, and I am not too familiar with friendships yet."

"It's okay, you're still learning, and I am still learning. It's a process," said Tracy. "You need to learn to start reading people."

"What do you mean by that?" I asked. I had heard the term 'reading people' before but never quite understood what it meant."

Reading people is like when your mother is having a bad day; you know not to go and ask her for anything or talk to her in the moment so she can calm down. It's those things, such as the vibes people give off, that let you know how they feel about you."

"Oh, okay."

"What vibe was I giving off when we first met?" I was very interested to know.

"I could tell that you were looking for friends the way you were curious to speak to everyone on the floor by the way your eyes were wandering around," said Tracy.

"Oh."

My reading of people skills was very weak, and the concept of learning to read people was like learning a whole new language for the very first time. If someone had asked me about what makes a friend, all I would've been able to say is someone who is willing and eager to talk to me and hang out. The concept of ingenuity was not something I would've known.

My naivete had been called out by others. Estelle shared with me that she thought I was very naive right off the bat from when she met me in Spanish class during that summer of 2002.

Estelle said, "I was afraid that people would pick up on how naive you were and really pick on you."

"What do you mean?" I asked. I wanted to gain knowledge and some clarity.

Estelle responded, "People take advantage of those who are naive."

"Oh," I responded. "How did you know I was naive, though?"

"I don't know how to explain it," said Estelle. "It's just a vibe."

Tracy and I had another conversation about a classmate from a class we shared. The classmate was quite a character, making loud comments and wisecracks during class. She often spoke of professors who were letting her get extended time on assignments and would tell stories of how she would talk her way to getting what she wanted in classes. Tracy and I were discussing the class and some of what the classmate used to say with regard to stories she shared and how she would get her way.

"Sonia, you know she is lying, right?" Tracy asked.

"Well, I only know what she said. I didn't think too much else."

"She's lying. Her stuff doesn't match up or make any sense. Gosh, Sonia, you should know how to read people by now. You are in college."

Even though Tracy meant well in the moment, Tracy had some of her own quirks that didn't come out in such a nice way. The one that stood out the most was how she got offended when I used to wake up around the same time she did. It was not like I did it intentionally; I was a light sleeper and would happen to wake up around the same time. One morning, towards the end of the Winter Semester, she just went off. I was still lying in my bed, just trying to relax and rest a little more.

Tracy noticed I was up and said, "Sonia, you're up. Get up!" She then asked, "Why are you always up when I'm up?"

"I just happened to get up," I replied.

"Well, you may not want to do this in the fall with your next roommate. She'll think you're watching her."

"I'm not watching you."

"I'm just giving you a heads-up," she replied and stormed out of the room right after she was done with her harangue.

That was enough to get me upset and irritated that morning. If I had enough time, perhaps I could have found the words to express how I felt. Even though people on the autism spectrum have feelings, they don't necessarily know how to communicate the words to their feelings at an exact moment. This is why social skills training, which also includes assertiveness training and how to self-advocate, is necessary.

What I would have liked to have said was this: "Why do you care if

I wake up at the same time? Are you paranoid?" This may have caused a bigger argument, but at least I would've let her know that she was out of line. Little did I know, she not only took issue with something rather trivial, but she went to Nadia and tried to complain that I was watching her change clothes. Nadia knew better than to believe her, and I only came to find out about it once the semester was over when Nadia complained about just how much drama she had to handle with the ninth floor.

The only other time Tracy complained to Nadia was when I asked her to lower the volume a little bit on her TV. I had an exam early the next morning, and I needed to rest, so I didn't go into the exam feeling tired. Tracy went to the TV room to finish watching her show. The next thing I knew, after I had come back to Chancellor Hall after studying at the library, Nadia pulled me aside.

"Sonia, I just wanted to ask about what happened with Tracy last night."

"What do you mean?"

"Tracy told me that she really didn't want to be bothered by anyone, not even you, at this moment. Something happened in her family recently, and she needs her space."

"Nadia, the only thing I asked Tracy to do was turn down the volume on her TV last night because it was a little loud. I had an exam this morning for one of my classes, and I needed to sleep as the exam was early. I never told her to turn her TV off or anything; I just wanted her to lower the volume."

"I understand that fully, Sonia. That is fair."

Towards the end of the Winter Semester of 2003, I started to feel really depressed. I was, first of all, overwhelmed with classes because some were particularly challenging. There was one professor I had for my Creative Writing class who was more rigid than what I would've thought a Creative

Writing teacher should be. He was picky about phrases I used in my stories and poems. I thought the whole point of Creative writing was to be *creative*. This would include being creative with dialogues, accents, phrases, etc. Also, everyone's work is completely subjective; who is to say it's good or bad? Art is art!

I hated my Constitutional Law class with a passion. I never really understood anything that was going on in there, even though I liked the cases about civil rights. I didn't know how to craft an argument for a 'brief' and didn't have the skills until later when another professor taught me how. All of it caused me great overwhelm because I had a huge portfolio for Creative Writing and a mock Supreme Court brief for Constitutional Law.

Even though the therapist was doing her best in working on letting me process my past, one thing we were neglecting was self-esteem work and therapeutic exercises that would've encouraged self-introspection. That way, I would've learned to be more comfortable with leaning into who I was and following my passion versus some version of myself where I felt I was running a never-ending race to catch up to. The disconnection with myself was a major vehicle behind what was driving this loneliness, apart from the fact I didn't really have many friends.

The emotions caught up to me to the point where I just lost it. The tears started rolling down my face, and as much as I tried to hide all the pain, I couldn't anymore. There were nights I used to spend crying on the stairwell because of all the loneliness, anxiety, frustration, discontent with what I was being pressured to study, and overall unhappiness with who I was as a person. The stairwell was a safe place to hide from having people notice me. Thank goodness nobody was running up the staircase for their workouts and were using the campus gym instead.

Nadia spoke to me briefly at her door. She saw me upset. I addressed the surface level: I was feeling lonely and disconnected from others. I told her how I felt like everyone else had a close friend or someone they could spend quality time with. I didn't quite have that.

Nadia told me, "Maybe you should find friends who have more time for you."

If it was that simple, don't you think that would've been taken care of? I responded, "It's not that simple. I don't know how to find such friends."

A saved-by-the-bell situation happened at that moment because Nadia's mother happened to call her. Nadia told me she would come and find me to talk more. I then walked toward the TV room, where I knew it would be quiet and I could have some alone time. Lucy, the girl who organized game night for the floor and the Valentine's Day girls' night, happened to see me on my way.

She asked me if I wanted to talk. We both went to the TV room. I caught her up to speed about how I had been feeling lonely.

"It's so easy to be caught up in the bubble. Tippecanoe is a bubble at the end of the day," said Lucy.

"Yes," I said. "Friendships are hard to come by around here. I don't have the kinds of friendships I see others have. It's so disappointing when you grow up lonely and are made fun of. I have a bad past of encountering bullying and rejection. I was really hoping for things to be different. I was hoping to feel more connected to others and have those friendships like I see other people on campus appear to have."

"Friendships are a lot like dating in that when you are working on yourself, things especially like dating come to you," explained Lucy. She then dropped the ball on me. "Well, I am going to be really honest with you. You make people feel really uncomfortable. You make *me* feel very uncomfortable."

"What do I do?" I asked, completely flabbergasted.

"You tend to invite yourself to things you aren't invited to," Lucy said.

"When did I do that? The only time I went out was when I got invited to do something such as the organized floor events," I said defensively.

"Sonia, there were other times when you invited yourself out. Some nights, you aren't meant to go out."

"I don't remember doing that."

"Well, anyway, don't you think you get a little too excited when you want to make a friend?" Lucy asked in a rather judgmental tone.

"Maybe. I didn't have any friends growing up, so I got excited about the idea of finally being able to have some friendships with people who seemed promising and nice."

"I think you tend to push people away from you rather than draw people towards you. You make people feel really uncomfortable to be around you, and that overexcitement that you have for friendships is a real turn-off."

I started to think of past behaviors. I, in good faith, don't remember ever inviting myself to join events except for one time when I asked to join Lucy on a trip to the store. I thought it would've been okay because we had brunch earlier that day at the nearby Indian restaurant that had a brunch buffet. She said I could come along, but in retrospect, it seemed like it was more of a forced 'yes.'

I would've rather been told, "I need some time alone." Perhaps there were some social cues I missed at the moment that made it hard for someone to understand why I didn't leave them alone. People had to be direct with me if they needed me to do or not do something. I wasn't always going to pick up on cues right away. The fact I was pushing people away wasn't a shock; after all, I proved it growing up in Forest Ridge and wore that ugly truth like a tattoo.

Chapter 17

FALLING OUTS AND NEW BEGINNINGS

Summer 2003 was one of the most liberating summers for me. I found the courage to eliminate toxic people from my life, including Janet. It all happened one weekend. Janet was living in an off-campus apartment about 10-15 minutes away. She saw me working out at the gym and came over to talk. She then asked towards the end of the short conversation if she could come over next Friday night and stay over. I didn't know how to tell her no, so I said, "Sure."

Something peculiar started to happen: I started getting bad gut feelings about that upcoming Friday. It was like my gut was screaming, "Cancel your plans now!" Of course, my own low self-esteem and self-doubt won over and pushed my gut feelings aside.

When Janet came over, she didn't seem to be in the best mood. One of the first things she said was, "If you want to get me something to drink, you can." I owed her from the time we went to a movie once, so we walked down to the Village, and I got her a Strawberry Shake. Even when we were at The Village, I noticed she had a snippy attitude.

Trying to make casual conversation, I said, "Guess what? I ran into some of our floor mates from last summer on campus."

"So?" That ended that conversation.

We went back to my room to hang out. After a minute, she said, "Put on some music. It's boring."

Luckily, I had a TV that could drown her out somewhat. The next day was when stuff really hit the fan. When I woke up, Janet was already up reading a book. "I've been up since 7 o'clock this morning. Is there any breakfast food around here?" The way she said it, I took her question to mean whether there was a cafeteria in the building.

"There is no cafeteria in this building."

"You know, in order to be a good hostess, you should have some food in your place."

"I have cereal."

"Well, can I have some cereal, *please*!" She seemed to be snickering.

As I started to pour her a bowl, she started griping. "I don't understand you, child. I asked you if there was breakfast food around here!" she exclaimed in an abrasive manner.

"The way you said it, I thought you asked for a cafeteria, I responded assertively."

"I asked if there was *breakfast food* around here!" Janet exclaimed, raising her voice even louder.

At that point, I had enough, and I told her, "Well, I thought you meant a cafeteria."

She then had it! She picked up the blanket she had borrowed, folded it, put it on my bed, and said, "You know, you don't even have to. I don't want it anymore. Here is your blanket. I will call you when I get home," in a pouty manner.

This was akin to how a child just throws a tantrum and storms off when they don't get their way. She then abruptly left the room.

Instead of feeling sad, I was relieved! But I was also angry. I didn't even bother to wait for her call. I didn't care if she made it home. In retrospect, I should've kicked her out the night before, but I had some decency in me. I didn't want to be blamed and looked at as the bad person should something have happened to her, even though I would've had my own defined reasons to kick her out. After she left, I celebrated because I felt so damn proud of myself. I treated myself to a nice meal.

I finally stood up for myself and spoke my mind. In retrospect, Janet was never able to handle when someone stood up to her, particularly those whom she felt she could use as a punching bag to take out the frustrations she had in her life. Janet used to complain often of being on the receiving end of racism. While I don't doubt she suffered and was in much pain and trauma because of racism, that did NOT give her the liberty to use someone on the autism spectrum as a punching bag.

Now, with Janet gone, the summer of 2003 opened me up to meeting other people through the courses I took. I also saw people I knew from Chancellor Hall during the summer on campus. I made a new friend, Savannah, through my Middle Eastern History class. I also connected with Tia, a Resident Assistant from Chancellor Hall, who was an international student from Brazil. I had met Tia earlier during the Winter Semester while she was working at the desk at Chancellor Hall.

Tia used to come over and watch TV often. I attended study groups for the first time that summer of 2003, and I learned that I do better studying alone than with others. As I was exposed to different people that summer, I learned increasingly about 21st birthday celebrations that other people were having or had. I loved hearing people talk about how they went out to dinner and the bars afterward with their friends. I thought I was making progress at having small talk with people that I knew, and I started to conjure up a birthday celebration in my head.

I started talking to people about turning 21 the first week of the Fall Semester, and people were already getting on board with it. Nadia and Tia were up for dinner at the Italian restaurant downtown. I told others I knew from Chancellor Hall about my birthday, and they told me they would be up for going out to the bars.

Tia even made a joke, "Sonia, I don't know how drunk you are going to get, but as long as we are not carrying you home."

We both had a good laugh, and I knew I wasn't planning on getting too crazy. I needed to learn about my limits and planned to go slow on the drinks.

I noticed that throughout the summer of 2003, my confidence started to build. I was working out a lot at the gym, I was looking good in clothes, and I was feeling hopeful and happy for what was to come. Before Sapna left for the summer, we got together, and she asked me to keep one of her bags with me so she didn't have to carry it with her back home. I agreed, and I thought for sure she would be in to celebrate my birthday. Sapna also said she was up for celebrating.

I talked to my therapist about my birthday. She warned me about not getting too overeager and overexcited because that can be a turnoff for others.

Dr. Theroux said, "Remember, Sonia, people don't like to keep hearing about the same thing again and again. Do your best to stay in the present."

The one thing Dr. Theroux encouraged was sending out a friendly reminder about birthday plans at least two weeks before so that people had it on their calendars.

In retrospect, the people I spoke to about my birthday were not close friends. A lot of them were acquaintances, people whom I knew from seeing them occasionally in Chancellor Hall and from events attended.

People who were saying that they would be about it, most often, were saying so out of common courtesy. I took people's words very literally and didn't think to connect the idea that people have to be close enough to you to celebrate you. I thought that people, because it would be an excuse to go out, would come. After all, that was some of the experiences I had where I went to a birthday party through invitation even though I wasn't part of the core friend group.

If I had to break this down even further, a majority of the people who said they would come out to celebrate me weren't really hanging out with me outside of class. I only saw Tia a handful of times when she came over to watch TV and sometimes grab food. I hung out with Savannah at the end of the Summer Semester when we went to grab food. It takes time to get to know someone, especially when people already have an established group of friends.

Day by day, I started building up the story in my mind of what the evening would look like. I would have a group of us go out to dinner at the Italian restaurant downtown. Afterward, we would go to the bars and just have fun celebrating together. I depended on this birthday celebration to finally feel a certain way about myself: Sonia Chand has finally arrived and is like everybody else now. This was only the beginning of the illusion.

Chapter 18

HAPPY 21ST BIRTHDAY! FISH SANDWICH AND CHOCOLATE SHAKE, PLEASE!

The buzzkill happened very quickly on the first day of the Fall Semester 2003. As much as the first day of the semester should feel like an ease, it felt more like a dead week before finals—people whom I spoke with kept backing out left and right. I saw Sapna at the computer lab, and she came by my room to pick up her bag. Sapna then let me know that she wasn't coming to my birthday at all.

Another big letdown was Tia. I saw her after class as I was walking back to my room.

"Hey Sonia, how was the break?" Tia asked.

"It was great. How about you?" I replied.

"It was a lot of fun. I took a trip to New York City."

"Oh, I love NYC! I went there for spring break my freshman year of college. I did a lot of sightseeing around the city."

"The city is beautiful. I did all the touristy things, such as seeing the Statue of Liberty, Times Square, Ground Zero, and Central Park."

"It was emotional to see the freedom lights. I had tears welling up in my eyes."

"Yes!"

"So, remember about Thursday!" I said.

"You know, Sonia, I will only come if I feel like it."

"Oh."

"Yeah, so anyhow, I need to get going. I will see you later," Tia said.

Then, I just lost it when I got to the lobby at Chancellor Hall. Nadia saw me and gave me a hug. I was having such a meltdown with the stress building up. Nadia assured me that she was still in and that she was going to try to get some of the other residents on her floor to go out.

My anxiety remained at a high, and I felt the cortisol build in my stomach. I was barely able to eat or concentrate. Deep down, I knew things were unraveling from what I had pictured in my head and led myself to believe would become reality. I couldn't have been more wrong. There were still social skills I needed to learn. I received feedback from Ankita, a floormate and friend from Chancellor Hall, about how I came across to people over the summer.

Ankita taught me how to go about helping a friend when in need. Ankita didn't appreciate how I wasn't too attentive one early morning when she was talking about hurting her foot. I was in a hurry to rush to an exam, so I told her she needed to go to the Tippecanoe Medical Center near campus. Ankita got upset with me around the same time I had a falling out with Janet. We ended up having a conversation about it, and she taught me I needed to use my words so that it didn't come off as dismissive.

"Sonia, it is understandable that you had an exam and were rushing, but the way you came across didn't come across right. A better way to address the situation could've been, 'I am so sorry you aren't feeling well. Is there anything I can do? I have an exam I need to rush to at the moment.'"

"Oh, I wasn't aware," I said.

"Sonia, it's fine."

At this point, I was breaking down in tears. "I am so sorry. I always feel like I am messing up in one way or another."

"Sonia, you are not alone. I had to have people guide me along the way at one point or another."

"Thank you."

"Another thing, Sonia, you need to learn how to start standing up for yourself and learn about other people and their boundaries. A lot of people on the ninth floor, unfortunately, didn't think very highly of you. As much as you tried hard to make conversations with others, some of the things you told them, truthfully, weren't their business."

"Such as?"

"Like, the lesson you learned about when Sameer didn't like you or when you told people you had never kissed before. That is none of anybody's business, especially if these aren't close friends of yours."

"Yeah, I can see. You should know that I have been standing up for myself to people. I just recently did that with Janet." I proceeded to tell Ankita the whole story of what I experienced with Janet.

Ankita was absolutely correct when she said, "Sonia, this should've been a friendship that ended a long time ago. It should've never got to where it had to get to."

In retrospect, I can see how having a lack of skills already put a dent in the way people viewed me. I cried every day on the week of my birthday. The Retro Metro had a gathering that Tuesday evening for a 'meet and greet.' I saw some people at the gathering, and one of the girls told me that it would depend on what her boyfriend wanted to do with regard to my birthday. That was enough to get me down in the dumps again after trying hard to remain strong and positive. I ended up leaving the gathering.

Unbeknownst to me, my parents spoke to the headmaster of Chancellor Hall and asked to oversee that I wasn't alone on my birthday. That motivated Nadia to throw a 'surprise birthday' in the TV room on my floor. I thought the intent was sweet, and Nadia did an amazing job organizing the gathering with my Resident Assistant, Hallie.

I started getting anxious when people asked about what I planned to do to celebrate the actual birthday. I told them what I had been assured of thus far. I was trying to hold onto hope even though I was holding onto a fantasy bubble that was about to burst. My anxiety prevented me from also putting in more effort to perhaps reach out to different people. However, all the rejections thus far had been a dagger at my chest.

All that I had conjured in my own head had already been unraveling. However, on that day in particular, it felt like a big blow. My family called to wish me Happy Birthday, which started the day as comforting. I did my normal routine of going to class and working out. I saw Leila first thing that morning as I was heading out the door to go to class. Leila told me she wasn't feeling well and wouldn't make it for my birthday. She didn't look well at all.

Phaedra and her friend were going to dinner early that evening, and she invited me to go along. At the time she was going, I had an early evening meeting. They were going to eat at 5:00 p.m., and I wasn't free till 6:30 p.m. I asked if she and her friend were able to wait, but they were starving. I told them to go ahead and eat.

Nadia ended up working that evening at the front desk at Chancellor Hall, so the whole dinner plan to go to the Italian restaurant didn't work out. My emotions were at an all-time high. I stopped by the front desk to see if Nadia was still able to make it out later.

She said, "Sonia, I spoke with the head Resident Assistant, and she told me that I can't go out with you to celebrate this evening. We aren't supposed to encourage alcohol."

I knew that was rubbish because I used to overhear other Resident Assistants talking about going out with their fraternity brothers, friends, etc. In retrospect, maybe Nadia didn't want to go out that night.

"Oh, that's a bummer!" I said.

"Yeah, but let me ask you, have you eaten?" asked Nadia.

"No. Not yet."

"Sonia, you should go eat. You could get very sick if you drink on an empty stomach."

"I have heard. I will just go pick up something. I am supposed to join my roommate and her friends at the bars."

I was feeling so hurt that things didn't turn out the way they were supposed to that I didn't have an appetite. There was a part of me that just wanted to become inebriated to forget all the feelings. The more responsible side of me said, "Eat something." I figured I would get something comforting and get in a good walk. I went to a fast food place and got a fish sandwich and a chocolate shake.

I feel so embarrassed as I write this. I mean, with all objectivity, this is an embarrassing story. You go to school with 40,000 students, and you end up alone eating at a fast-food restaurant for your birthday dinner. All of what I heard about others, such as group dinners out and then going to the bars as a group, were not things that happened to me. It was a big letdown, and it was a letdown that I somewhat did to myself.

As I was biting into the fish sandwich, I felt so ashamed and embarrassed. Flashbacks of all my social experiences back from elementary school till the present ran through my mind like a movie on fast-forward. I thought about the fact that perhaps even classmates didn't, aren't, or wouldn't be doing what I was doing. I finished the sandwich and took the chocolate shake to go. I was walking towards the building, and I started to just break down and cry, cry, and cry. The emotions of overwhelm and upset took over like a tidal wave that would just knock me down.

Things eventually turned out for the night when I went to Beats for their mixed drinks special. I was trying to navigate hanging out with the people I went with and also finding the new people from class who said they would be interested in celebrating because they were planning on being at Beats regardless.

Savannah ended up having an emergency meeting with her sorority, so she said she was going to try to come out once things got resolved. Savannah taught me about sorority life over the summer during the time we got together for lunch. The sorority house was very rigid, and meetings were mandatory.

I got lost in the overload, the sensory lights, the surround sounds of beats, the music, and just people everywhere when I got to Beats. My roommate told me I should drink more every time I went by her and her friends. I took her advice. I wanted to down the drinks to forget the fast-food dinner. I wanted to forget the harsh reality that I, in fact, celebrated with strangers and was not part of the friend groups that I saw other people have. I heard birthday celebrations being shot out by the DJ over the stereo. That felt like a bee sting each time that night, and no amount of alcohol was able to drown that out. I got a ride home with some people who lived in my building whom I didn't even really know. I felt bad about myself, and being around others who had tight friend groups I wasn't a part of only made me feel ten times worse.

Chapter 19

DEPRESSION, TOXICITY, AND GROWTH AND CHALLENGES

The Fall 2003 Semester was numbing and depressing, and every day felt like I was struggling to stay above water. The feelings I developed the night of my birthday of anger, hurt, betrayal, and self-loathing were hard feelings to shake off. They clung to me like an octopus clinging to a face. Sometimes, I would start with tears welling up during class. It also didn't help that birthday conversations were happening right, left, and center around me. People were going on trips with their friends for their birthdays, people were going to dinners, and having parties that they were excited about. None of which would've included a fish sandwich until after they were done for the night of drinking and needed the grease, perhaps.

Dr. Theroux used to reinforce the idea for me to 'pull myself out of the depression.' She also used to validate feelings, and she told me, "Sonia, I think anybody who was in a similar situation to you would also feel devastated to feel that nobody was close enough to celebrate them."

I became a toxic person in the meantime. Dr. Theroux encouraged me to speak up to those who hurt me. I eventually gathered the courage to tell Tia and Sapna how I felt. Tia apologized for her behavior and acknowledged that she was selfish. Sapna never apologized. If anything, Sapna made me feel bad for calling her out.

"Sonia, my cousin was visiting me in town, and I couldn't just leave her alone. And I am always going to put my family first. Secondly, how well do you even know me?" Sapna said.

"I thought we started becoming friends this past Spring Semester."

"That is the thing: we were just barely scratching the surface of getting to know each other. You barely know me."

As I reflect on it, that was a pretty crappy way to handle the situation. Also, if Sapna had an issue with the fact we really didn't know each other all too well, then why did she leave her suitcase with *me for* a summer? Sapna had a best friend whom she could've easily left it with.

Something peculiar started to happen though throughout the semester. Sapna used to encourage me to come and vent to her about what was going on. I would do it, and at times, I would cry out of frustration at the way things turned out. I hated myself first and foremost. I was emotionally dumping, but simultaneously envious that she had friends despite sharing her own difficulties in childhood. Sapna emphasized how hard she worked to get friends. I kept thinking to myself that I was doing the same thing, and that was aggravating for me. The anger was more of my own frustrations I needed to work through.

I also needed to work through all the pain that went beyond the surface of being embarrassed and ashamed of eating at the fast-food place for my 21st birthday dinner. The embarrassment and shame traced all the way back to childhood.

Sapna and I would make plans throughout the semester to hang out at some point over weekends. Most often, I would be stood up. This caused me to feel quite bewildered because I didn't quite understand why Sapna would encourage conversations for me to be vulnerable to her yet stand me up. I missed the social cue that it wasn't a genuine friendship, but rather, I needed to look at her more like an acquaintance. In retrospect, we were both unhealthy in our own ways, and I had no business emotionally dumping on Sapna. My pain was my responsibility to bear, and it was not to be dumped on someone else. For that, I apologize.

What really needed to be worked on was more processing of the past and how that affected where I was at the time. I needed to learn how to heal, and I needed to learn how to love myself. I hadn't the first clue on how to do that.

Dr. Theroux kept normalizing my feelings by repeatedly saying, "Anybody would have felt like you— devastated."

She used to reiterate for me to "pull myself out of the depression." I tried so hard but couldn't. I didn't have the skills. My emotions ate me up every day, and I had major crying outbursts when I was alone.

The intense depression lasted for the whole Fall 2003 Semester. The only times I felt somewhat 'normal' were when I hung out with others at the bars in The Village. I finally felt like I was being part of the group even if that was just a facade.

It was not until the Spring 2004 Semester that it finally started to click on making friendships that would stick for longer. I got a new roommate in the 2004 semester, and Sapna graduated.

Leslie arrived in the room after I left to hang out with Savannah and her friends for a little bit in the Village. Leslie studied to be an actress and worked in theater on stages in NYC for a few years before coming back to Tippecanoe to finish her degree in computer graphics. Leslie and I were both startled by each other's appearance that night. We each thought we would have the room to ourselves, but nonetheless, it was great to meet her.

She woke up upon me turning on the room lights, and we had a brief conversation. She was making wise cracks at my expression of intense hunger that I had while I was munching away at my food. Leslie said things in such a way that her comic side clearly showed!

Leslie and I went to the mall together the next day because she needed to buy some things for the start of the semester. She and I had lunch together, and we had a great conversation. I shared with her about being on the autism spectrum. Leslie shared the story about her sister, who has mild intellectual impairment. Leslie's sister was treated horrifically in school, and Leslie reminisced over the feelings of intense anger and devastation from watching how her sister was mistreated.

Leslie asked one question that stood out to me: "Were you misdiagnosed a lot?"

That question hit hard, and even though I didn't realize it at the time, it was the million-dollar question that showed somebody understood and knew.

Throughout the spring of 2004 and into the Fall Semester of 2004, it was a process of learning how to make healthier connections with others. There were times when people got annoyed with me, and I got yelled at by others because of my ignorance of how I was coming across.

My interest in joining a sorority started to grow during the Fall 2003 Semester. I thought if I was part of one, I would finally learn something from others about how to be likable and have friends. There were times I used to see girls who were members of sororities dressed to the nines with nice outfits, hair done, and makeup on. I used to wish I could look like them.

Savannah and I had a few discussions about sorority life, as she was part of one. I never realized how often I brought up sorority life until she called me out on it.

"This is why I get so irritated every time I talk to you! You always talk about sorority life," exclaimed Savannah.

"Oh, I am so sorry! I didn't realize," I said, feeling really horrible at that point.

"It's just that nobody really talks about sororities much anymore. I mean, I am about to graduate. Nobody even brings up sorority stuff anymore," explained Savannah.

"I understand," I said. "I really didn't mean to keep on going on about sororities."

"Sonia, I get it," said Savannah assuringly. "I know you wanted to be a sorority sister, and I understand your reasoning. It's just that everybody is past that stage, and nobody brings up sorority stuff much anymore, especially since people are about to graduate and move on."

"I get it. Once again, I am so sorry," I said.

I took that experience with Savannah as a learning lesson as to what I can improve on moving forward with her and with others I would interact with.

I eventually made another friend whom I was able to connect with in a deeper and more intellectual way: Carrie. We met at a Salsa party on campus, and I recognized Carrie from seeing her around at Chancellor Hall. Carrie was an avid Salsa dancer, and a stellar academic graduate student studying electrical engineering.

During the course of the friendship, she taught me that it was okay to call her to have lunch on weekdays. Carrie led me on how a friendship could work, and that is through being more consistent in communication. My only idea of friendship at that point was that people hung out on weekends. I didn't realize that the idea of friendship ran deeper.

Carrie and I connected on deeper levels of pain in that she and I shared a similar tormented childhood. She was on her way to a healing journey, and she introduced me to the book *The Four Agreements*. I enjoyed seeing Carrie on her healing journey. She used to vocalize lessons she learned through her experiences. Carrie used to say how she used to talk a lot, almost hogging over conversations, to compensate for past trauma and anxiety. She also admitted to shutting people down due to her own struggles with her mental health. I was able to fully appreciate her realization, and it inspired me to dig deeper within myself. It would take years before I was able to learn how to fully realize how to be self-introspective and go deeper to heal myself. The therapy I got at Tippecanoe University scratched on the surface, and the therapist started to go there with me when discussing the past. It felt good to let it out, but nothing was done in depth.

Carrie and I kept in touch after we graduated, and I visited her in Los Angeles before starting law school that summer of 2006. We had so much fun together when I visited her, and that was the highlight of my entire summer, above and beyond anything else. We went to Warner Bros. Studios and took a tour. We got to see the set of the popular TV show back then, *ER*. We also saw the exterior set of *Gilmore Girls*. I got to meet up with Savannah while I was out there because she was visiting family. We all went to the beach, and it was such an amazing memory to be able to visit friends and have some fun.

Carrie and Savannah's friendships were a testament to how never giving up and allowing myself to continue to strive to make connections had its rewards. However, the real connection that was missing was the one I had with myself. I graduated college feeling a void, all because I knew I was about to enter a career I didn't have a sincere heart for. Even though I would've still had my challenges socially, I could bet that the edges of the loneliness and the overall college experience would've been better enjoyed if I had listened to my own heart. That would've meant allowing me to explore psychology or journalism—courses I would've enjoyed much more. In taking courses I enjoyed, I would've felt and become more connected to the most important person: myself.

Chapter 20

LAW SCHOOL HEARTBREAK

GRADUATION WOES, INTRO TO INGHAM, AND CRUSHES

Before attending Ingham Law, I stayed home for a year and a half post-graduation. I graduated a semester early from college in December of 2004. In the meantime, I moved back to my parent's house to study for the LSAT, work at a law office, and apply to schools. Working at the law office only confirmed that I didn't belong in the legal profession. I didn't necessarily enjoy the work, and I didn't present as my best self. I was stress-eating bad foods. Case in point, I used to go to the convenience store down the street and get mini donuts and diet soda each morning for 'breakfast.' The food acted as comfort as I was reading negligence cases online to prepare briefs for the attorneys. I used to see a therapist once a week as more of a liferaft to help me get through the transition period before launching to law school.

I acted very insecure and ultra-sensitive at work. I tried to be the comedian for people at the office because I loved to listen to the way they laughed. I was displaying qualities that were antithetical to what a person would perceive an aspiring attorney to be by a long shot.

Even though I went to work every day, I used the job as a way to crave approval because I was very lonely being back in Forest Ridge. I didn't know how to tell my parents I didn't want the legal field as a profession, especially since it was hard-shoved down my throat that I would become a lawyer. I didn't do well on the LSAT and got rejected from practically every law school I applied to except for one: Ingham Law.

Ingham Law School had a liberal admissions policy in that they accepted those who had lower-end SAT scores. However, there was a catch: the school operated on a year-round basis and was one of the toughest law schools in the entire country. The grading scale already started at a C-curve. There was a certain academic GPA you had to hold in order to keep enrolled at the school. Ingham Law School had two years of mandatory core courses students had to take, whereas other law schools only had one year. The competition at the school was fierce, and just passing and not being on academic probation was a victory in and of itself.

As difficult as it was, the two years of mandatory courses paid off when it came time to take the bar exam. Because I already had knowledge of the subjects, I didn't have the added burden of having to actually learn the topics.

I had already noticed at law school orientation how people were already connecting and forming friend groups. How does a person do that so quickly? I had a meltdown from being too overwhelmed at orientation with all the newness that hit like a tidal wave. For one thing, I was being thrown into a completely new environment. I was embarking to study at one of the toughest law schools as someone whose heart wasn't fully in it, and I was around a lot of people and socialization.

I didn't come off as the best start at making friendships. For one thing, I lost the skill of learning how to make friends, which I finally started to understand somewhat towards the end of undergrad. I was slow to make friends in law school. When people got to know me, the one thing that stood out that people thought was odd was the fact that I never dated anybody.

The summer of 2007, which was the final semester for my 1L (first year of law school), was when I started becoming more social. I connected more with people whom I met at orientation, namely Khloe and her neighbor Natalia. Khloe used to notice me studying all the time at the library. She was big on getting study groups together, and she invited me to join a study group she was hosting. I thought I would try a study group again, despite not having the best experience with one in undergrad. I eventually learned the hard way that I do better when I study by myself, as studying with other people can get overwhelming.

The way I grasp information is through seeing it firsthand. When other people are involved, it gets too much for me with the talking and getting distracted. Like anything, not everything is for everyone. Some people thrive in study groups; I was not one of them, and that's okay.

I was sitting in the car with Khloe and Natalia after we were done grabbing food one evening. They were talking about their dating lives. Both girls had boyfriends. They started to ask me about my dating life and whether I had ever had a boyfriend. I told them I never had a boyfriend, let alone been on a date. Khloe and Natalia were flabbergasted. They weren't the only ones flabbergasted. Other classmates mentioned there was a big part of social life that was missing in not dating. I was aware of that without having to be told.

I used to feel like I was missing out, and sometimes, those intrusive thoughts crept in that a relationship was something I never had. The feelings of missing out on the guys I had crushed on stung hard. I used to notice that even after they had broken up with people they were in relationships with, they were able to move on and date someone else. I was amazed at how people were just able to move on, whereas I struggled to get someone out of my mind once a crush developed.

I was always brainwashed to believe that I would get set up by my parents for someone. However, arranged setups don't necessarily guarantee a marriage. People have to like you first. You have to have that 'it' factor. I didn't have that factor and was nowhere even close to even having it. Also, you never know why people will marry you. People could marry you for the wrong reasons, with the main reason being for money. What a person really needs more than anything is genuine love; someone loving someone for who they truly are. I felt I had to try my whole life to be loved and accepted; that was not another battle I had the energy to fight.

Despite comments about my singlehood, I managed to have fun that summer of 2007, and I was introduced to karaoke for the first time.

That summer of 2007 was the first time I started to notice someone very handsome. Demetrious used to nod and smile at me when our eyes made contact. I didn't really know him at all, as we weren't in the same classes during my first year of law school. However, things changed in the fall of 2007, during the fourth semester, when he happened to be in my Estate Planning and Succession course.

Demetrious sat on the far left side of class but towards the front of the row, at least five rows up. I was in the middle section of the room, towards the top. I sat by people I got to know from being at the library.

The more I saw of and got to know Demetrious, the more he acted flirtatiously. Demetrious would, at times, either pat me on the back or do something weird with my chair that was kind of like a shove but still felt like a fun flirty hit on the back of the chair. I started to really get hooked on him.

Khloe and Natalia encouraged me to get his phone number. I was super scared to even ask because I was afraid of getting laughed at. I clung to past memories of how guys treated me before, not realizing I wasn't the same person I was back then.

Natalia found me in the library and called me out on behaviors she noticed, not only with Demetrious in terms of not getting his number but rather how I acted around the whole group. She noticed that I was backing out of things at times at the last minute.

If I backed out, it was due to sensory issues and overwhelm. I needed to learn how to communicate that better. I didn't share with anybody I was on the autism spectrum up to that point out of fear of what people might say or think. In reality, I was afraid of hearing, "If you have autism, you shouldn't be in the legal profession."

I knew I shouldn't have been in law school or the legal profession, but it was because of my lack of passion or desire for it rather than because I was with autism.

"Sonia, honestly, people are rather annoyed with you," Natalia said. "You can't make a good decision and are not a good decision maker. How do you expect to be successful in this field? In order to be a lawyer, you have to make a good decision and go with it," Natalia explained.

"What do you mean?" I asked.

"You told Khloe that you would study with her, but you never made it. She was waiting for you at times."

"I didn't realize," I said.

"Well, a lot of times, you act indecisive. It kind of gets annoying for others and frustrating," Natalia said, sounding exasperated.

"I didn't mean to," I said, feeling bad.

"Another thing, why do you keep on talking about Demetrious if you are unwilling to do anything about him?" asked Natalia.

"What do you mean?" I asked, bewildered.

"You need help in talking to guys," Natalia stated.

"How?" I questioned.

"You need me to help facilitate how you get a guy's number."

"I think I can do this," I said, feeling somewhat insecure.

"No, Sonia. I don't think you will," Natalia said in a doubting manner.

"What do you mean? I asked.

"I don't think you will get his number, Sonia. Look, you haven't gotten his number so far."

"I don't know how," I said, once again feeling insecure and lacking, as if I was behind on milestones. It's like I was placed in a cohort where everybody knew how to use the toilet, whereas I still needed to learn how to be potty trained.

"That is why you need help," said Natalia. "Everybody knows you never had a boyfriend, there is a lot of shame in that, and that you would never ask for his number. Every relationship starts with a conversation. When I met my boyfriend, I wasn't even supposed to be at that bar that night. But I happened to bump into him at the bar, had a conversation, and look where we are today."

"Oh," I said.

"Life is going to pass you by if you keep living in fear the way you are living," said Natalia.

"I know," I said, feeling hurt.

"Also, I heard your grades weren't that good this last semester," Natalia pointed.

"No, they weren't," I said.

"Well, how badly do you want to be a lawyer? You could always be a paralegal," Natalia said.

I got so hurt by that comment that it took every bone in my body to not really want to speak my mind and tell her my thoughts. I really wanted to say, "You are being a cunt ass bitch. Back off!"

"I am doing what I need to do," I said, holding back tears.

The conversation finished, and I left in tears. I called Khloe and asked her to meet. We sat together, and I told her about what was discussed. I apologized for my behavior. Khloe was understanding. I also told Khloe and Natalia about the autism diagnosis, eventually.

Natalia then said, "It makes sense why you didn't get Demetrious's number yet."

It's sad that it was all Natalia could focus on instead of looking at the bigger picture of the struggles somebody on the autism spectrum faces. Not getting a guy's number is only a small slice of a big pie.

I eventually asked Demetrious for his number after I remembered how a classmate asked people for their phone numbers for school-related matters. I asked Demetrious if I could have his number to discuss a topic in Estate Planning, as I didn't attend one of the makeup sessions after class had been canceled. It coincided with another course I had going on.

Demetrious and I met for a 'study' date, and he went through some of the material. Before the date, Khloe took me to get my hair done. She took me to a place where she knew people who worked there. The place was mainly made up of students attending the cosmetology school who were getting hands-on experience. Khloe's friend was attending the school, so she trusted that other people were as diligent and talented as her friend. Unfortunately, that didn't end up being the case. The person who ended up doing my hair cut it in a way that made it look horrible. Khloe, fortunately, knew what to do.

Demetrious took notice when I walked into one of the rooms he blocked off at the library for the 'study date.' He noticed when I walked through the door about my hair, "Wow, your hair!" he said.

After the study date, my crush and feelings for Demetrious only grew deeper. I started texting him at the end of the semester. He had a final exam the day after my last final exam. I texted him the night before his exam and told him I wanted to see him. However, I went out to celebrate the end of the semester with a friend and had to leave the next morning for home.

When we got back from the winter break, I saw Demetrious at the library as he was walking in. I was standing in the lobby, ready to head to a class. I gave him a hug and kissed him on the cheek. He was like, "Aww, thank you."

This made my heart melt even more. That same week, the first week of the semester, Khloe suggested that I ask Demetrious to dinner to catch up on our respective winter breaks.

I sent Demetrious the text, but I didn't hear back for three days. When I told Khloe about how I hadn't heard back from Demetrious yet, she told me that she didn't think Demetrious was into me.

She was right. Demetrious sent me the text three days later where he said, "Thank you for the invite to dinner, but my schedule is kinda crazy right now."

That was where he had left it. I remember telling Khloe what he said.

She said, "From a friend to a friend, this guy is not into you. If he was, he would've brought it up to accommodate another day and time for you. The fact he could tell you 'no' in only the first week of the semester is also a red flag."

"Do you think I should suggest another day and time?"

"No, that is his job to do. He already told you he is not into you by the fact he didn't even bother to suggest it in the first place."

"I don't get it. Why would he act so kind and flirtatious and then turn me down?"

"Because he's a d***," Khloe said.

"Oh, okay."

I still didn't understand right away everything that happened. I never understood the disconnect between actions and incongruent subsequent behaviors. This was a total twist in the maze that I didn't see coming.

I tried to explain to Khloe how I had never had a boyfriend and how I was rejected quite often. She told me that I had to give guys a chance. She was referring to her friend whom she wanted me to go out with. I thought I had given guys a chance, and I was doing the best I could. I asked her friend to grab dinner without it seeming like too much pressure. I mentioned the word 'friends' as part of the context of how I thought we could start off this dinner.

At first, he seemed okay with it, but then he called and left a snarky voicemail the next day: "I just am calling to let you know that dinner is canceled tonight. *As friends,* I don't think that should hurt you too badly. Also, *as friends,* perhaps I will see you *with friends* another time."

"You could've just given him a date, Sonia!" exclaimed Khloe.

This conversation should've been a clue that this was the extent of the support and understanding I would ever receive with regard to this situation about Demetrious. Khloe just used to get irritated around the subject of Demetrious.

"He doesn't like you!" would be echoed time and again. Khloe got irritated enough to one day just let me have it. "Look, Demetrious doesn't like you. No matter how many times you get shat on, you will just keep going back to him. You like jerks, and you don't believe you deserve better!"

That hurt a lot! However, Khloe was right about going after the jerks. I didn't have a good foundation with relationships to begin with, so I was just going for what I knew. In my mind, the way Demetrious acted towards me with the chair hitting and flirtatious behavior was the closest thing I ever had to a guy acting nice to me at that point.

In an effort to try to get more support and make more friends, I connected with some other people I had classes with during my 1L year: Jade and Claire. I became friends with Jade first. Jade took a 15-credit course load which afforded her the opportunity to take the Summer Semester off. We connected once she came back to start the 2L year.

There was a welcome back party for Ingham Law Students at a bar further away from campus at the start of the Winter 2008 Semester. Jade invited me to join her and her friends, so would all go together to the welcome-back party. I was excited to hang out with them.

We met at Jade's apartment first and had a toast to starting a new semester before heading to the party. The first party was just people hanging out with their groups. There was music, but unlike the previous welcome-back party, there wasn't a whole bunch of people dancing. I managed to shock people at the welcome-back party by doing an impersonation of my ethics professor.

On the first day of class, my ethics professor rolled on the floor as a way to prove a point: 'You've got to roll with the material.'

And, in case you are wondering, this is NOT made up. *This is too good to be made up!*

I did the exact same impersonation of the professor in front of what

I thought would just be a couple of people watching it to what ended up being a whole group of students.

People were flabbergasted, mouths agape, eyes wide open! Someone asked if I was okay. I told her I was just doing an impersonation.

My friends and I stayed at the welcome-back party for a little while before we decided to go downtown to the bars near Ingham Law School.

I saw Demetrious at the bar we ended up at. He was with his friends, and they were all standing around a table. I had enough alcohol in me to just come on strong to him. When I came on strong, I kept kissing him on the cheek. I was desperately looking for an answer to why I got rejected. Akin to how it was with other guys I have crushed on, I wanted him to tell me what was 'wrong' with me and that he felt the need to reject me. I was looking to him to try to 'fix' me that night.

The bar was too loud to even facilitate such a discussion, nor was I in a mental space to even be able to digest it. However, I was just looking for him to at least say what was wrong with me. I was looking for the whole, "Sonia, you are disgusting, you are ugly, you are annoying, you are filthy, you are stupid, etc."

I guess I was thinking that the reasons people gave me in my younger years for why I wasn't accepted or liked were the same things that were happening in law school. I had underestimated that I outran that version of myself by numerous milestones.

I ended up staying at Jade's apartment after we had all left the bar. When I left the bar, I had sent Demetrious a text saying I needed to speak to him. My phone ended up dying on me. Mind you, back in 2008, I had a Sprint Sanyo Katana phone. It is nothing like the iPhone, or other advanced technology smartphones people have today. Safe to say, my phone didn't charge fully until the next morning.

I had received two texts from Demetrious. The first one said, "You said you wanted to talk. Are you okay?"

The second text I received was a complete blow to my feelings and self-esteem, "Your friends are hot!"

I was depressed for days afterward because it triggered me from when I was younger and was called 'ugly.' It made me believe that perhaps I was 'disgusting' and something was horribly wrong with me.

I used to cry every day throughout the semester, and a lot of my conversations with people were meant to decode male behavior. I kept asking men, "What does it mean when a guy leads a woman on and then doesn't go out with her?"

Of course, everyone had their opinions. Some guys would say, "Maybe the girl misread the signals that he was just being friendly?" Other people said, "He was just keeping you on a string to play with you so that he has somebody, or he never really liked you to begin with."

There are so many reasons why people behave the way they do, and it was confounding at times to figure out others, let alone guys. The more I tried to figure things out, the more depressed and confused I started to feel. In the meantime, my parents found a therapist who agreed to do phone sessions with me. His style of therapy wasn't quite the fit for what I needed at the time. I needed someone who was more of a conversationalist and could talk me through things.

I felt like I was alone and thought, "How come I wasn't liked whereas everybody else seems to be getting dates? How come everybody else has it so much easier conversing and connecting to one another, and for me it feels like an uphill climb on Mount Everest?"

One professor, Dr. Davidson, extended his grace to me when I visited him during his office hours a couple of times. I disclosed about being on the autism spectrum. Dr. Davidson disclosed about his daughter having a disability. She had been tested for autism spectrum disorder, but she was found to not have that. Instead, she had another disability. It was touching to hear Dr. Davidson's story about his daughter, and it was very apparent how much love he had for her.

One thing that really stood out to me was when he said, "My heart hurts for her."

Another profound statement he made to me was about how he noticed people's lackadaisical attitudes toward the law and found many people were there to just check off a box instead of having a passion for jurisprudence. What he didn't understand was that I was fitting that exact same type of person.

On the weekends, I definitely was drinking to excess as a way to numb the pain. I went to McKelly's Karaoke Bar with Khloe. I sang and danced to "Jump" from the Pointer Sisters. Next thing I knew, that became a thing. Khloe had a whole group of her friends come out to watch me do the song and dance, and of course, it was met with a lot of laughter.

Natalia had a birthday dinner mid-semester. The group met at a Mexican restaurant and bar not too far from Ingham Law. That night, I made up a raunchy rap for people, which, yet again, was another way to channel my pain.

I reached out to a family friend, as she and I were close at the time. She was just like everyone else in that she just said, "Brush it off, get over it, move on."

What people didn't understand was I *was* trying to move on. I never felt like I fit in; I was not like the other girls who were getting dates and experiencing short-term relationships. I was also dealing with past trauma pain that resurfaced. There was a lot of healing and self-introspection I needed to do that wasn't being done. I didn't have the tools back then.

Furthermore, I didn't have self-esteem nor have the tools to understand how to build myself up. After all, I was never really put in positive environments where I was able to thrive.

I went to Dr. Patel for a medication consultation to see if perhaps there was a pill that would just help me move past all the pain. None of the medications he prescribed to me were a fit, and if anything, they made me feel like a zombie. I even tried going back on Lithium, the same medication that I got put on in sixth grade and had to take twice a day. The Lithium made me feel drowsy all day. I knew I would never pass my classes if I kept on that medication because everything was like a fog under them.

It seemed as if each day that I was trying to hold onto hope for a better day, the dimmer it became. There was a girl I knew who showed me her arms one night after we had left a bar. We were discussing people and relationships. She told me to always think good about myself regardless. Otherwise, it hurts badly. This was when she disclosed her self-injurious behaviors via the form of cutting. Her arm was quite scarred from it.

I thought since I didn't have people who understood me, I wasn't in a place where I belonged to begin with; I was practically screaming only for it to be heard by deaf ears. I felt I had no other options left to try to not feel the internal pain anymore. The tipping point to the suffering was when I saw friends walking arm in arm with guys, looking as if they were going somewhere to chill out. I had just left the library, and I decided I was going to try to cut myself to see if the internal pain would go away. Please note that I was not taking it as a means to attempt suicide.

I went to the store and bought cutting knives meant for the kitchen. I took one out and went right into my room. I sat on my bed, and I faced towards the mirrored closet. I am a right-handed person, so it was significantly harder for me to do a whole lot on my dominant arm. I did cut some, though. However, when it came to my left arm, I went to town with the cutting, all while tears were streaming down my face. It hurt each time physically, but the physical pain felt soothing in comparison to all the mental pain I had been wrestling with.

Cutting didn't fix how I felt inside, but rather, only shifted the pain to my arm to sting for a couple of days. The shower was brutal the next morning, for sure! The long sleeves came in handy for the weather we were having at the time, as it covered up all the marks. There were at least 20 marks on my left arm and 8 marks on my dominant arm. I would roll up my sleeves when I was alone, and I saw at least 28 marks of sorrow, 28 marks of pain, 28 marks of trauma, 28 marks of frustration, 28 marks of confusion, and most of all, 28 marks of a very lonely, lost, and hurting woman who was in desperate need of redirection and guidance in life at large. Cutting was not the answer nor the best choice to make, but that was the only thing I knew to do at that time with what I was given.

If I could go back and say something to my younger self, knowing what I know now, I would tell her that she is fine the way she is. She is beautiful as she is. She is not the mistreatment and rejection from others. Some people are just jerks because of their own shortcomings in life, and that has nothing to do with the bright and beautiful Sonia.

Chapter 21

POST SELF-INJURY THERAPY
JOURNEY TO DR. GREY

My parents ended up coming towards the end of the semester to pay me a visit. Throughout the semester, I complained to my mom about watching everyone else get a date and how I was always the girl on the outside looking in. I shared about feeling rejected by Demetrious. My mom didn't necessarily know how to handle my feelings of rejection. When my parents came to visit, we all went to dinner at an Italian restaurant in the downtown area 15 minutes away from Ingham Law School. During the dinner, discussions came about regarding my lackadaisical attitude towards school. I revealed my arms to my parents.

My parents insisted I go back to this therapist I saw locally near Ingham Law School the summer before. The therapist was okay overall. She was telling me the truth of why I was unhappy in law school.

She said, "We all have an assignment we have to do before our time is up on Earth. If you are feeling unfulfilled in a career path you are on, and it is more than just one bad day, then perhaps this is not your assignment."

I was too scared at the time, but she was telling me the truth that I needed to hear and admit to myself instead of living the brainwashed lie of a version of who I thought I needed to be.

The therapist was good at helping me understand human behavior to some level. One important thing she used to say is, "People know whom to target and go after. It's like how sharks are able to detect their prey. People go after those whom they feel they can go after. There is a vulnerability about you that you carry around. You need to make sure you keep your head held up high and stand up for yourself. If people talk about dating issues and are harping you for not being like them, you need to learn to start saying 'that is not up for discussion.'"

The therapist also taught me another valuable lesson when it comes to men: "A man who flirts with everyone is *not special*. Gosh, if I were to be intimate with him, I would make him wear double rubbers."

We both laughed. She continued, "No, but seriously, with a man like that, you could only speculate where he has been."

Where things started to take a turn was when the therapist used to say things such as, "You aren't meant to have friends right now, you aren't meant to have a boyfriend, or you could've had a boyfriend years ago."

Statements like that were made throughout the sessions, and I felt like the comments were dismissive of the real struggle it was emotionally and socially for me to be able to connect with others.

Toward the end of the Winter 2008 Semester, my parents attended an autism meeting in Chicago. At that meeting, there was a keynote speaker, Dr. Grey. Upon first impression, my parents were very impressed by how he presented information about the autism spectrum in terms of certain behaviors and social blindness. Dr. Grey spoke of the repetitious patterns of behavior with those on the autism spectrum. My parents found him to be very informative and knowledgeable, which, in turn, led them to attain his contact information. Sure enough, I was soon sitting in his office.

Chapter 22

NICE TO MEET YOU

SONIA, YOU NEED TO DROP 15 POUNDS

I was excited to finally meet Dr. Grey after I was inundated with all his praises from my parents. I had an appointment with him right at the start of the Summer 2008 Semester. It was on a Saturday afternoon. We did the normal intake process of him asking questions and getting a background history. Dr. Grey examined my arm as he wanted to see if there were scars left over from the cutting. At that time, my arm was healing from the cuts. You could see the marks, but they were becoming faint. It was yet another reminder of how much pain I was in and my desperate attempt to escape the pain.

Dr. Grey made some good points during the first session. He explained that sometimes when people don't know how to describe something or explain how they feel around a person, they can be quick to label a person as 'weird.'

"Unfortunately, many people on the autism spectrum get accused of being 'weird' because people don't understand some of their behaviors and thought patterns. We are going to have to do some detective work as we are starting to figure out what particularly is coming out from you that is pushing others away and causing you pain and difficulties."

"That sounds really good. I finally feel like someone understands me."

"I have extensive experience working with the autism spectrum. I should tell you, Sonia, that my youngest son is on the autism spectrum. He was diagnosed when he was three. He has challenges that he still faces, but because of his early diagnosis, he was able to progress a lot more for his age than people who weren't able to get diagnosed in early childhood."

"I can definitely understand that one. I wasn't diagnosed until I was 20. You see where it got me."

"I am here for you, and we will work through this together."

"Thank you so very much. I appreciate that."

"Sonia, we will meet weekly for now. We can even do sessions twice a week to start with."

"I would appreciate twice a week."

"Noted. We will talk on the phone, and if there are weekends you could come to the office, I would encourage you to come in. Now, I wanted to address the self-injurious behaviors you were doing. Do you still have urges and thoughts to cut?"

"No, I don't. In fact, I have been working on getting better physically alongside mentally. I have been going to the gym almost every day. I have been trying to get back into running and have been doing weight lifting."

"That is great. You really could benefit from dropping 15 pounds."

At first, I didn't think much of this comment. Little did I know that it would serve as a catalyst for future comments that dealt with more weight and body image. If I had known better, I would've called him out the first time and told him his comments were not only derogatory but professionally inappropriate. After all, inappropriateness only leads to further inappropriateness.

Chapter 23

NAVIGATING THERAPY WITH DR. GREY WHILE HANDLING TOXICITY ON A 'FRIENDSHIP' LEVEL

During the summer of 2008, I started noticing Demetrious's roommate and best friend, Jerry. Jerry was also a tall, handsome man. He had sandy blonde hair and ocean-blue eyes. In fact, every time I looked at him, I would envision the middle of the ocean with the sunlight beaming on the waters. Jerry was also charming and kind to people. It wasn't long before I started crushing on him. Like Demetrious, he wasn't interested in me.

I think Jerry came to find out about my crushing on him through people. I wasn't shy about sharing how I felt about him—the pain of not being liked never changed.

Dr. Grey started the second session I had with him by saying, "I wonder if perhaps there is a sign you are wearing that is pushing people away."

"I don't know how to explain the reasons behind why people behave the way they do towards me. All I know is that throughout my life, I have been met with a lot of hatred and animosity. It didn't just end in childhood, and once I graduated from high school, the rudeness persisted in college and even some here."

"This is where we need to do some detective work and get some feedback from others that could help us. Do you know some people whom you could get feedback from?"

"I think I do."

"Why don't you start working on trying to get some feedback?"

"Okay."

It would take a while before I would get some feedback. In the meantime, I would have a harsh reality every time I went out to the bars with people. I was always the girl that was ignored when I was out. This set me up to want to drink more as a way to compensate for feeling othered and inadequate. The drinking only led me to act out in ways that set me up to become a laughing stock to many because that was the time when I would go and perform the raunchy rap. I would also hit hard on men who were repulsed by me.

There was one man (and, this is me being nice to even call him a man instead of a little bitch) in particular who just gave me dirty glares after a time I tried to be playful and flirty. This is the same man whom I came to find out from one of his female friends that he would go around saying to people, "Why do you talk to Sonia? She's so weird."

I found this to be quite saddening for the fact that it was coming from somebody in his 20s. The last time I heard this kind of phrase was when I was in middle school from people in their early teens.

Jerry, like Demetrious, never really wanted to be my friend in any way, shape, or form. He kept himself at a distance, more so we were acquaintances. I used to express my concerns to Dr. Grey about what I used to witness of others and how I wasn't living up like other people in terms of dating and interactions with the opposite sex.

Dr. Grey used to say, "Well, it is odd for people your age to never have gone on a date, but it is not odd for someone with autism. I have known many people even older than you who haven't had a date."

"Really?"

"Yes. There are people, though, on the other hand, who really worked on themselves and found love, too. I think you have a chance at finding someone, and we are going to need to come up with a way for you in the next five years to increase your chances of finding someone."

"That sounds good. I hope I can find someone."

Later, throughout the year, my parents set me up on an Indian dating site. It was not worth a minute of my time. For one thing, I was not too much into Indian culture by then to think of it as enough to necessarily want to marry someone because they are Indian. Jade looked through some profiles with me, and I wasn't really interested in the people there.

There was one profile we came across where the guy even stated, "I expect the woman to stay home with children and give up on having her own social life once she becomes a mother." I was taken aback by how controlling, degrading, and oppressive that was towards women.

I was reinforced by people like Claire, who would make comments like, "You're going against your parents by looking outside your culture. Things were different for your brother because he is a male. Things are different for females."

Even though the part of things being different for my brother because he was a male was true, that didn't mean I was confined. Claire had her own ideas of what it meant to be an Indian woman, based on what information she got ahold of that was disseminated and gave off the wrong picture.

Claire was somewhat like Khloe in that she wasn't as patient or understanding when it came to how I reacted in what people would consider emotionally immature ways to rejection and being treated the way other girls were.

The way I behaved was by expressing hurt and pain from feelings of rejection. I would get upset when I felt rejected and express frustration.

Claire didn't understand where my reactions were coming from. She used to say, "Your dating skills are like that of a 15-year-old girl. You're better than that."

What was better, though? Sometimes you don't know what people went through in order to be where they are, whether it's someone successful or whether it's someone who is socially delayed in some kind of way.

"I wanted to punch you" and "It just pisses me off" were other phrases I used to hear from Claire. She would be referring to the conversations I had the night before with her and Jade, where I would express misunderstandings about feeling rejected and overlooked by guys compared to female peers.

Claire wasn't able to understand why I felt the way I felt.

As far as dealing with Claire, I should've told her, "If that is how you constantly feel, then don't be my friend. I will be fine with or without you in my life."

If I had more confidence the way I do today, I would've said it to her back then. However, there was a part of me that admired Claire, even despite how nasty she could be. A part of me gravitated towards her because I wanted her and Jade to make me into a Barbie girl. I used to despise who I was because I didn't feel it was okay to be me. I was looking to be fixed and changed. Both Jade and Claire had the looks and a way of attracting people towards them.

There were some things that Claire suggested in terms of makeup. She told me about the natural look being in, and she suggested that I start buying eyeshadows that were in the brown shades.

Dr. Grey suggested that perhaps there was a way I was using body language. Also, Dr. Grey discussed sex appeal and how perhaps other women have learned ways to use that to their advantage. I didn't have the first clue as to what sex appeal even was.

Dr. Grey gave some suggestions, such as "Keep up with the latest fashion trends, makeup, and weight management."

Dr. Grey's wife worked as an image consultant and psychotherapist. Dr. Grey set me up to go shopping with her so she could teach me fashion styles after we had an in-detail conversation about the idea. I thought it would be good since I had developed enough trust in Dr. Grey.

My mom joined along for the ride, but she was strict about what I was able to purchase in terms of bottoms. She protested against me buying skirts, even pencil-style, because she didn't believe I would know how to handle a skirt.

Mrs. Grey and I were able to come up with an outfit. It was an orange cardigan, a matching scarf with a pop of pink color to it, and a shirt that went underneath the cardigan. I also bought a pair of black pants. The outfit we picked out together was the best outfit I owned at that point.

I started experimenting more with makeup in the Spring 2007 Semester and continued until the end of law school. Mrs. Grey gave me a mini eyeshadow palette that was more neutral in colors. My makeup was never done correctly in the sense that I would put on too much. People could've easily interpreted that as me 'trying too hard.'

Dr. Grey used to talk about social blindness with people on the autism spectrum. "A lot of times, people on the spectrum don't understand how they are coming across to others. There may be things they do that people don't connect with in terms of communication. Maybe it's the way you, Sonia, have told jokes or the way you laugh that may come across as offensive or just weird to some people."

Dr. Grey eventually picked up on the fact that my walk wasn't a fluid motion at one of the in-person sessions. I had a herniated disc during one of the sessions from going too hard all at once at the gym. Even though some of the reasons why my walk wasn't fluid were due to the fact I was in immense back pain, my walk wasn't also fluid based on the fact I had a funny gait from when I was in early childhood. I have glimpses of memories of walking on my tip toes as a child. I was never fully comfortable walking with my whole foot on the floor. People have called me out on my walk before throughout my life, but nobody got into specifics of what they saw. All that was said was that I walked 'weird' or too fast. I knew I walked fast at times, and I was unaware of my posture. Dr. Grey suggested finding a modeling school to attend courses to learn to fix my walk. I would eventually learn how to walk properly with the shoulders back and upright posture once I finished law school.

Jade and Claire noticed before that I was a messy eater. I was having pasta with them at an Italian restaurant after shopping one day, and the sauce kept splattering out of my plate when I was eating. I could see how this could've been a turn-off to people, especially because people who are going into such a prestigious profession such as law would be held to a standard to have impeccable table manners.

Dr. Grey worked with me on some Cognitive Behavioral Therapy techniques, such as challenging and reframing negative thoughts I used to have. Dr. Grey taught me to say to myself, "Just because I never had a boyfriend doesn't mean I am nothing." And, "Just because I was told mean things about myself doesn't make them facts."

I was taught to challenge cognitive all-or-nothing distortive ways of thinking, such as the 'all-or-nothing mindset.' "Just because you never had a relationship or struggled to find good friends doesn't mean that this will be the case in the future. Things can change as you continue to grow and learn how to soothe yourself and as you continue to develop more into yourself."

Dr. Grey emphasized that I had additional challenges other people didn't have to deal with because of being on the autism spectrum and having a comorbid mood disorder.

The environment I was in didn't contribute to my well-being by any means. Claire and I were having constant misunderstandings, but when times were good, they were great. In retrospect, I could never trust Claire to stay consistent. Claire was super-protective over the fact that I was still a virgin, whereas the vast majority of women my age were clearly not.

She used to say, "You better not have sex until you're married." This was Claire's way of asserting power and control.

I should've asked her, "Why do you care if I am a virgin or not? Kind of odd for you to be that obsessed with someone you consider a friend, no?" This was another clue that it was time to end this friendship with Claire.

I had a lot of resentment built first and foremost towards myself, then my family. The resentment I had towards myself drew from the fact I felt once again like I was a failure because I felt I was trapped in a life I didn't want career-wise. My heart was not in the material, even though I continued to study hard with struggles.

I was unknowingly putting up with toxic friendships because I felt trapped and didn't value myself enough to voluntarily end them. I was clinging to what I thought I needed in order to survive being in the place I was.

I resented my family for making me stick through a place where I didn't belong despite desperate attempts to try to explain why I wanted to leave. All my dad used to say was, "You make yourself like it."

My mom also didn't support my desires and used to enforce that I stay in law school. I used to say that I felt I picked the wrong career choice and would be better suited for becoming a therapist to help others, especially those on the autism spectrum, to feel understood and heard. She would tell me, "You're better off in law school instead of trying to see where else you could be a fit."

Even though I couldn't force myself to like law school, I learned, instead, to like self-medicating and numbing through drinking. Not only did drinking help me escape from myself, but it also helped me check out of an environment where I didn't fit in.

Dr. Grey was another person who used to discourage me from quitting law school. In fact, he thought I shouldn't even be in the mental health field or a trial lawyer because of autism and the possibility of people not connecting with me. He thought I was best suited to advise people financially where people would connect with me on a matter of expertise. My heart was more suited to helping others in different ways—ways that would help heal and inspire. I wanted to be that person for someone else in ways I wish I had that someone for myself.

WEIGHT, WEIGHT, WEIGHT

"So, you were never known as the heavy child?" asked Dr. Grey to start one of the sessions.

"No, I was not. I may have been a little overweight in middle school, but that was due to my binge eating from all the bullying and not knowing how to handle such intense emotions."

"There is a way you think about and use food," he stated.

"I know. I am working on it."

"Maybe you need to start adding some strength training to your routine."

"I have been."

"Something isn't working if you have been going to the gym as often as you say you have been going."

"Well, people have been noticing and telling me I have been looking gorgeous. Girls, that is."

"They are just trying to be nice to you. Perhaps you need to start eating more lean meat and more protein-based foods. Another thing, hire a nutritionist to help you."

"Okay," I replied.

"The reason I am telling you all this is that with your autism and mood disorder, everything has to be perfect. Thin girls get away with more."

"I see."

Some of what Dr. Grey said about how I thought about and used food was correct. However, the whole pushing of body image didn't make me feel good. There were other times when Dr. Grey was instructional and supportive but critical at other moments. I didn't realize at the time how I was beating myself up with even harder jabs based on things that were said in my sessions.

I shared some feedback I happened to get that a couple of people told me throughout law school. Apart from that one guy telling people I was weird, there was another girl who was going around echoing the same sentiments. It is no surprise that those two were friends, and they happened to be in the same friend group as Demetrious and Jerry.

Dr. Grey would say, "Well, let's listen to what these people are saying. You should care about what people say about you because this is what carried you throughout your whole life."

The times when Dr. Grey showed some support were when I discussed feeling hurt from rejections and the overall misconceptions people had about me. He also supported me when family members felt it was their place to think, "Well, Sonia is in law school now. She is 'cured' from autism."

That couldn't have been further from the truth, and just because people go to graduate school and pursue professions doesn't cure them of autism in the least. I struggled to pass my classes, and there was a semester when I was placed on academic probation because I just didn't connect to the material. I had to retake a course that I failed. Ingham Law School allowed for one retake if you failed a course, and they would void the course upon successfully passing the retake course.

There were family members who also felt I should stop therapy altogether. In truth, therapy was the only thing keeping me afloat, even though the therapy sessions weren't always the best.

"Sonia, that really irritates me that they say things like this about you. If your family members were serious about entertaining such a thought of you completely ending therapy, they should seek consultation from someone who is highly acclaimed in the field. I personally don't feel you should stop therapy. If anything, I think it will damage you."

"I agree with you, Dr. Grey. I feel that therapy has been supportive in some ways in that at least someone understands autism." This was where I blinded myself into thinking everything was okay with these therapy sessions: the fact that somebody understood autism.

"Sonia, you are getting some real therapy that has teeth to it."

"Yes, and I feel you understand me."

"Believe me, I do," I replied. "What would you say to the guys who rejected me?"

"I would tell them, 'I don't know what kind of a girl Sonia would've been for you. However, if you would've given Sonia a chance, even if it is just to get to know her, I think that would've really been a great opportunity for the both of you.'"

"Aww, thank you. That means a lot."

"Sonia, I mean every word of that."

Overall, the majority of the therapy sessions for as long as I was in law school were a vacillation between supportive and critical. Some of what Dr. Grey said would be contradictory to his previous statements.

On the one hand, he would say, "Because of your autism and mood disorder, everything has to be perfect. This means you need to be thin. People these days are obsessed with all the airbrushing, and I have clients who won't date a girl who is even five lbs overweight."

All I could respond with was, "I am doing my best. I get it."

Then, he would say, "On days you feel bad, you need to learn to go do something for yourself, such as go get an ice cream."

Mind you, these statements wouldn't have been said in the same session, but yet the messages were contradictory.

I would share about certain situations that would come up at bars when I was out with 'friends.' Dr. Grey reminded me of those moments when I was left to my own devices, moments when I saw people go off and dance with one another, moments where I was pushed to the side whereas other guys and girls were chatting away to remind myself that 'I am still beautiful, I am still loveable, I am still worthy.'

"Sonia, the unfortunate truth is when people have any kind of psychiatric diagnosis, others don't like to be around that person. People step back," said Dr. Grey in a judgmental tone."

"That's unfortunate," I said.

I was bamboozled by how judgmental a psychotherapist could be towards those with mental health issues. These are people whom Dr. Grey was supposed to help, and it was his job as a professional to help them feel safe. How he was able to comment on people who struggle with mental health was not only a way to push people away but was completely unprofessional. It made me wonder why someone like him was even a psychologist, but like in any profession, people can enter it for the wrong reasons.

"I know about that all too well, I said," remembering flashbacks of my youth.

"That is why you need to make sure you are doing things you enjoy. People want to be around someone who has sunshine in their hearts. People don't like to be around people who have all sorts of issues," he said.

"I am working on it," I said, feeling judged.

Dr. Grey's lambasting about looks hit hard. "You are better off going for someone who perhaps is a 7 out of a 10. I don't think guys see you as more than a 7. You have a pretty face, and if you lost weight, you would look better overall. However, you aren't a movie star."

"I think I am beautiful the way I am," I responded.

This was one thing I started teaching myself when depression hit hard during the Winter Semester of my 2L. I used to practice saying, "I am a sexy diva," repeatedly in front of the mirror. At first, it felt very weird, but it became a routine and something I grew to love saying to myself.

"Guys don't see you like that," Dr. Grey said.

"I don't care what guys see me as. It's the opinion of myself that should count first, Dr. Grey."

There was no response for that, and rightfully so! Ultimately, it's how you view yourself that counts the most because you are with yourself all the time. Make your view about yourself a good one! Also, Dr. Grey was no supermodel-looking male, so he really had no business instructing me on how I should look. The only thing he had going for him was his wife, who was gorgeous. Hey, this is a spade calling a spade.

Chapter 24

TABLE MANNERS TIME

Before law school graduation, I did an internship at a prosecutor's office. My brother was diagnosed with stomach cancer right as I was entering my third year of law school. He, unfortunately, didn't survive having cancer, and he passed away on May 21, 2009. My heart hurt for him during my last year of law school, which also played into some of the drinking I was doing. My brother's passing was at the time I was just beginning my internship, and it was a process in and of itself to take some days off up to and after my brother's passing.

I also had to do an independent study in order to graduate on time, so I was kept rather busy over the summer. My mom was in touch with an organization in the suburbs of Chicago that dealt with services for autism. The lady who ran the organization, Mrs. Gorman, had gotten to know my parents in the early 2000s, post-diagnosis. My mom happened to call Mrs. Gorman to discuss some of the social challenges I was having. Mrs. Gorman suggested that we meet with one of her employees, Kelly.

Kelly, my mom, Mrs. Gorman, and I all met for lunch, and Kelly introduced and described the kinds of work she does. Kelly studied psychology at a graduate school in downtown Chicago. Her goal was to focus on individuals with autism.

We came to an agreement that Kelly and I would spend time together, and she could give feedback on what she saw that may be preventing me from coming across as the best version of myself.

Kelly and I met for the first time by ourselves over lunch. She was able to get an assessment of me the first time we all met, and she noticed that my motor skills were off.

"Sonia, the first thing is you need to eat slowly. Remember this rule: two bites, one sip of water, two bites, one sip of water."

"Okay."

"I also noticed the first time we met that you were doing something with your fork that was different from what other people were doing when they were eating. It was like you were making a noise with it when the fork was hitting your teeth. Your grip was also off."

"Oh, I wasn't aware."

"You tend to use your fork as a spoon at times. Let me show you how you properly hold your fork so that it goes to your mouth. I want you to watch me, then follow."

I watched Kelly closely and took mental notes. I repeated to myself two bites, one sip of water.

"Sonia, we are going to focus on eating because when you first start dating someone, that is what you are going to be doing."

I was receptive to her help and support. However, it felt quite embarrassing that a woman who was in her mid-20s had to be taught table manners. Such table manners were taught to people at substantially younger ages.

Dr. Grey was in full support of the work I was doing with Kelly. He used to even suggest, "Have her watch you stand up, sit down, walk to the bathroom, walk around, etc. We have spoken before about your walk being 'off,' so I am glad you are getting some help with that."

"Thank you," I said.

The next time Kelly and I met, she noticed how I played with my hair a bit when we were at the table. Kelly taught me to keep my hands together on my lap the moment I felt like fidgeting with my hair. This is still a work in progress, as I have a tendency to fidget with my hair for sensory regulation. Kelly saw improvement with the two bites and one sip of water. She also noticed an improvement in how I held my fork.

I started mentioning to Kelly some of the concerns brought up by Dr. Grey about my gait being off. Kelly mentioned that she may have seen something and she would be on the lookout. She initially focused on table manners and motor skills when it came to eating.

I was usually quite flexible with where we met, but there was one place she set for us to meet where I didn't get a good feeling. I looked at the menu online, and the items they served were not to my taste. With reluctance, I asked her if we could go somewhere else, a spot we hadn't been to before, but I knew the menu would be much more to my liking. She agreed, but her unhappiness showed when she came to the place.

"Sonia, don't do this again! What would've happened if you had done this on a date?" Kelly asked scoldingly.

"I don't know," I replied.

"Your date would've probably been pissed off and annoyed," said Kelly.

"Oh."

"Please be mindful of that moving forward, and don't do that again," said Kelly sternly.

"Yes, sorry about that," I said.

A part of me wondered if Kelly was bothered by my changing the place because she really wanted to eat at the other restaurant.

During the dinner, Kelly noticed that I ordered only an appetizer that wasn't the most nutritional in value. She taught me the whole concept of making sure I order healthy foods when I go out to eat.

Kelly said, "Eating healthy shows people you care about yourself and take care of yourself."

Kelly addressed my walk after she saw me walk up a flight of stairs to use a restroom. She had me practice climbing the stairs with a more proper form. Kelly and I went to the mall so she could see how I walk around places. Kelly was then able to show me how I was coming across when I was walking, and it was definitely not a fluid motion by any means.

Kelly taught me to walk standing up straight with my shoulders back. She showed me how to walk from heel to toe, using the whole foot in a more fluid motion. Apart from working on the walk, she used to give constructive feedback on appearance. Kelly never commented on my weight. She, instead, commented on how my hair appeared disheveled and that my bra needed to be a better fit. I was taught to start paying more attention to those aspects before I left the house.

In the short time that I worked with Kelly, she taught me the things I needed to start to work on to improve myself. I found working with her to be more helpful than attending sessions with Dr. Grey.

Dr. Grey, on the other hand, kept harping about weight and appearance. He would, at times, say, "You know, there are times when there is not that someone for everyone. A lot of people battle with loneliness."

Dr. Grey would talk about how he had clients who were never able to find someone. He kept on his serenade about how some of his clients wouldn't go out with women five pounds overweight.

I finally had enough and asked him, "Don't you think it's possible that these clients who are fussing about women being five pounds overweight are just being shallow? Women can pick up on men who are shallow and will keep their distance." After all, pigs are for eating, not for dating.

Chapter 25

SONIA C TAKES ON NEW YORK CITY

LAST DITCH EFFORT IN LAW

In a last desperate attempt to try to like the legal profession, I looked into Master of Law programs (LL.M.). I was working at the same law practice where I worked back in the summer of 2005 upon passing the bar exam. I wasn't feeling any moment of working there. I was also informed I wouldn't be getting paid unless I brought in my own clients. That was the statement I needed to just check out completely.

From a social standpoint, I wasn't feeling it in Chicago. For one thing, when my brother died, my parents allowed a friend of the family to interfere way too much with our family. It was getting to a point where he was starting to cause friction in the family; I would get yelled at because I wasn't living up to the family's vision of what I should've been. In their mind, I should've been working at a prestigious law firm and finding someone to settle down with. I was doing neither of those things.

The family friend used to call my parents constantly and ask, "Did Sonia find somebody? Did Sonia find somebody?"

The family friend got involved in setting me up on Indian Matrimonial Advertisements, but I wasn't interested in the people on there.

For one thing, the people weren't even near but in different cities, states, and even countries. Another thing, I wasn't going to marry someone solely based on the same cultural background, especially when stigmas run high about things like mental health and the autism spectrum. I didn't have any more energy to fight another battle and prove why I should be accepted. I was tired from trying my whole life up to that point.

On the social front, it got kind of lonely at times. I managed to make some friends, but it was only few and far between when I got to see them. A lot of people were busy moving on in terms of partnering up and getting into serious relationships. There were friends who had their families here, and they were tied up with family obligations. I enjoyed the time when I saw friends, and we would have a lot of fun. I took some of my alone time to build up my health and fitness. I worked out with a personal trainer for the very first time, and I ran my first 5k. I took classes in Improv because I thought I would try a hand at stand-up comedy. After all, people used to tell me I was funny in law school and should try comedy.

I used to tell people while I was in law school that I wanted to be in the arts, like being an actress or a comedian. In comparison to how it was in middle school, the rejections and other feelings I felt in law school pushed those daydreams of what it would be like to be a famous comedian. What would it feel like to have everybody know your name? Would I feel like I arrived and was accepted because I finally made it big? What does it feel like to have millions of fans know your name, buy your tickets, and, most importantly, come and cheer on YOU?!

I stuck around for a few months of Improv, but what I think I probably would've enjoyed better was an acting class. After all, if I was going to be the girl who was considered 'weird' and subsequently outcasted, I might as well make the quirky personality work for the greater good, right?! Hello Hollywood!!!

In the midst of trying to find myself, I eventually made a good friend whom I was able to hang out with. I met Maya at the building gym pool area, and we started talking about popular TV shows that we enjoyed watching. Maya was one of those people you felt safe with, that you could be your whole and true self around her. Maya and I were able to have in-depth intellectual conversations. We were both growing in our own ways and figuring out who we were and what we wanted out of life. Maya and I went to a concert where she announced her job transfer and move to NYC. Even though I was sad to see her go, she started convincing me to move out there, too.

Over the Thanksgiving holiday in 2010, I visited some schools while visiting family in NYC. I got to catch up with a couple of people I knew from Ingham Law for dinner the first evening I landed. I also saw Maya while I was there. She showed me around a little of the city. While I was staying with relatives in NYC, there was a spark in me that just whispered, *"Sonia C., you need to move to NYC!"*

The first thing I started to do when I landed back in Chicago was start looking at LL.M. programs in NYC. I got accepted into a program for financial services at a school in Manhattan. I also started to study for the NY Bar Exam, so I could practice. I moved in April of 2011 to NYC, and the excitement I had when I first moved to the city of magic and wonder was something unlike anything I had ever felt before up to that point. I finally felt I could become the person I wanted to be without feeling like a bird with clipped wings. However, there were major hurdles and challenges along the way.

THE BREAKDOWN THAT CHANGED EVERYTHING

When I first got to NYC, I took the bar examination preparatory course. A majority of the summer of 2011 went into studying for the bar exam. I met people at the prep course, and in fact, I reconnected with someone I had met at Ingham Law School. I remained focused, for the vast majority, leading up to the bar examination. It was not until after the bar exam was over that things really started hitting me hard. For one thing, I was back from always having something to do to having nothing to do for a brief period. I always thrived by having things to do and not having anything to do, which, in fact, did the exact opposite for me.

I tried to remain occupied during my free time by going to places like Central Park. I went to a speed dating event I found off a MeetUp site. The speed dating event didn't go that well. I didn't find a connection with the type of people that showed up. There was one person who was there whom I thought was decent, but I didn't pick up on the fact he was not really checked in. I knew he got on his phone at times during the event, but everyone got on their phones. For me, I thought he was being like everyone else.

I had a discussion with someone after the speed dating portion of the event was over. He noticed how I was interacting with others. He noticed how my way of reading people was wrong.

"I noticed how you were interacting with people. Something is a little off about you."

"How?" I questioned.

"The way you kept trying to have conversations with people who were clearly showing you no interest."

"What do you mean?"

"The guy you were trying to talk to. He was clearly not into you."

"We had some conversation."

"Okay, but he got on his phone. His attention was elsewhere, and I even saw him looking around the room at other women."

"Oh."

"The way you read people is wrong. You are a lost puppy."

"I am not lost."

"Yes, you are. I hate to break it to you, but you are a lost puppy."

I left the event feeling bad about myself. My mom always told me, 'Truth is bitter.' As much as I hated to hear that kind of comment from someone who was able to pick up on what he saw from me, I hated the fact that I was always the problem. I was lost, lonely, scared, and worried about the future. The 'what ifs?' were rampant in my head. "What if I didn't do well in the LL.M. program? What if I am not successful because I have not been successful thus far in my legal career? What if I am left all alone, never finding love? What if everyone else gets to celebrate milestone events with the person of their dreams, and they build community with many friends like how I saw happen for many relatives and with some friends but I am left all alone? What if I am so alone I die? Would anybody even notice enough to care? Would people even remember who I am?"

I knew I needed to change something within me, but I didn't know what to change. In order to combat some of this anxiety with a desperate attempt to quiet these ruminations, I went to the bar alone and sadly drank to excess to the point where I got cut off from being served. This was only the beginning. The feelings kept festering until the start of the LL.M. program.

The real breakdown happened at a birthday celebration that a person I thought was a friend at the time put together. She and her sister invited another girl to come out, whom I thought was a friend until after that night.

Before that night, I had thrown a post-hurricane/belated birthday celebration. The original date of when the party was supposed to have been at an earlier date, but the party had to be moved due to Hurricane Irene. On the night of my birthday party, I was trying to have fun. I didn't realize I had become a sloppy drunk. I thought I was having a good time and encouraging others to have fun and let loose. After all, we had all undergone surviving a hurricane.

It was not until the next time we went out that I knew I was not in a good headspace to even be out. I remember having coffee with a family friend before at a hotel to catch up. We had good laughs. I already had been feeling anxious about going out, and I should've listened to my gut feeling to stay home. I was afraid of disappointing my friend, Stacy. Stacy and I had a family law class together at Ingham Law School, and we connected on one of the weekends while the whole school practically would be out at the bars.

Stacy invited her sister, Sally, and another classmate, Susan, whom we knew from Ingham Law School who graduated with us, to come out to celebrate my birthday. When we got to the place, I could tell Susan already had an attitude. I knew some energy was off, and I didn't know how to run away from it. It also didn't help that the girls were talking about guys and having experiences with intimacy. Susan had a boyfriend. Stacy and Sally spoke of a hurricane party they threw where they had guys let them know they were attracted to them. Those were not my experiences, and I was already feeling insecure and bad about never being able to live up like my peers were able to. I tried to escape the bad energy by doing what I knew how to do: drink it away. That night, I was also taking drags of cigarettes, which I barely ever did. I knew I wasn't in a good headspace. If I could rewind time and redo that night, I would have stayed home and made an excuse that I wasn't feeling well.

If I hadn't felt the energy, I could've made an excuse to leave the place early and go enjoy myself at home. Sometimes, you are better off enjoying your own company than being around people where there is unease and tension. I tried to talk through it with Susan on the ride home after, but she wasn't having it. She said she would call me in the morning.

I was so upset that night that I took solace in finding a group of doormen that were sitting outside a building. They happened to see me upset while getting out of a cab, stumbling. I went to them and cried my eyes out. I basically told them my life story, the feelings of rejection, feelings of emptiness, loneliness, and loss. The doormen who first laughed seeing me were the first to comfort me. We must have talked for at least a good 45 minutes. By the time I got to my apartment, it was 4:45 am.

I was not able to sleep when I got to my apartment, so I went for a walk down near the 9/11 memorials. 2011 marked the 10th anniversary, so there were quite a bit of people milling around the area early that morning.

I was still not in the best state of mind. One man, who was part of a church group, happened to make eye contact with me. He said a prayer for me after I also shared with him everything that had been going on. I hope for anybody out there, especially if you find you are all alone crying your eyes out without support from friends or loved ones, that somehow grace comes and finds you. I just hope that it isn't when you are left alone and feel like you can't be in the corners of your own walls in the wee hours of the morning, but rather grace comes and finds you much sooner.

When Susan called the next day, she was anything but supportive.

"Listen, Sonia. I am worried about you."

"I understand," I said

"You need to go to meetings or go see somebody," said Susan."

"I am aware," I said.

"Honestly, it is uncomfortable being around you. Your birthday party, especially, was a disaster. It made me feel uncomfortable watching you," she said.

"I was just having a good time and encouraging others to have a good time," I said.

"You may have been. You were also sloppy, a sloppy drunk," declared Susan.

"Susan, I remember that night clearly. I was having fun and encouraging others to have a good time."

"I had a great time with everybody, but I didn't like how you were acting. That is why me and my boyfriend left."

"Sorry you felt that way," I said.

"I can't be friends with you if you are going to be this way. It's not fair to have this kind of burden on others."

"What kind of burden?" I asked, feeling judged, insecure, and horrible about myself.

"The burden of talking about your issues, then trying to drink them away. It's not fair having that burden around others," said Susan.

"I am not trying to be a burden. I acknowledge I am going through a lot and feel stuck between a rock and a hard place. I am also on the autism spectrum, trying to do my best."

"You can't use your autism as an excuse for everything," said Susan in a snarky manner. (This is an ableist comment)

"I am NOT using my autism as an excuse for everything," I said in a defensive manner. After all, that was a low comment to use someone's autism as a strike against them when they've already fought millions of battles before a person has even met them or behind the scenes when nobody is around to watch or support them.

"Also, don't put me on a guilt trip for not hanging out with you," Susan said in a chastising manner.

"What do you mean? What are you talking about?"

"The time you called me on the night of fashion week and left me that voicemail!" exclaimed Susan.

"I wasn't putting you on a guilt trip," I responded.

"You said I was abandoning you," said Susan, disappointingly.

"I was just joking."

"My dad tells me I am abandoning him, and I see him three times a week. I didn't get to choose my family, but I can choose my friends. I *chose* to be your friend. Out of the many friends I have, I see you the most," said Susan, sounding as if she was obliged to be my friend.

"I appreciate your friendship, and the last thing I was trying to do was be a burden," I said, even though the emotional pain I was feeling was throbbing hard.

"There is so much more I can say to you, but I know that you are in a really bad state. I don't want to hurt your feelings," Susan said. As if some of what was said already didn't hurt enough.

The rest of the day, I just felt numb. The voices of past statements from therapists rang loud: "You're not worthy of having as a friend," what Dr. Shah said, or another time when Dr. Grey said, "It's easier to dump on people who are on the autism spectrum. They hold a lower status on the social hierarchy, so don't be alarmed if you get dropped easily."

What Dr. Grey said, unfortunately, had a lot of truth to it. What Dr. Shah said rang in my head so loudly that it was to a point where I tried my hardest not to be that person whom she said made me unworthy. I didn't want to let people in on my pain, but in doing so, I was recreating another situation where I was doing exactly that. However, the only place to go when you are down is back up. Even though I wasn't proud of what I had done as far as drinking to excess as a way to numb my pain and unease towards situations and, *most importantly, myself,* the breakdown I had only allowed me the opportunity to rise up stronger.

THE COME UP

I found a therapist who was practicing right in Midtown Manhattan. Her office was not too far from the Empire State Building. Dr. Forrester was an expert in autism spectrum disorder, and she mainly worked with people on the spectrum.

I liked how inquisitive Dr. Forrester was right off the bat. She asked me how I would socialize with others when I go out to places like the bar. I told her about how I try to be the jokester for others, especially when I have been drinking. I explained to Dr. Forrester that I took improv classes in Chicago in an attempt to try to become a stand-up comedian. She pointed out that I was missing the major social cue of acting on stage versus acting ordinarily, as a person would around other people non-performing.

Dr. Forrester and I worked on handling how I behaved around other people, especially when they were in a couple's setting, and showing public displays of affection. I told her I acted normally and tried to enjoy the experience, even if it was uncomfortable at times to watch public displays of affection. She explained that I might make a painful face or show some discomfort that could make others around me feel uncomfortable. Dr. Forrester and I worked on a rap battle to be used internally for when I felt othered or reminded of rejections. *"Hey, enemy, you say nobody likes me, and I was a loser. Yo, let me tell you I got my mom, I got my dad, I got my relatives, I got my friends."*

At the time, I was working with Dr. Forrester; a friend, Roseanne, whom I met in the elevator, called me upon hearing of my breakdown. Roseanne was a fashion consultant and was the CEO of her own company. We agreed that she would help me fix up my wardrobe and teach me the skills on how to dress up.

Because I didn't have a lot of clothes in my closet, to begin with, she didn't have to spend that much time in my apartment. We went to the stores not too far from my house. Roseanne reminded me of an important lesson, one that I learned back in speech class from high school: "People know if they are going to like you within two seconds." *First impressions mean everything.*

Unlike the first time I ever worked with an image consultant, Mrs. Grey, I was more free this time to try whatever I wanted and to try different outfit combinations. I tried on blazers, dresses, skirts, pants, cardigans, and scarves. I bought a few outfits that I could mix and match. She took me to a shoe shop to buy boots.

For the first time in a long time, I actually felt like I was beautiful. I was excited to get dressed up for the day. I glowed on my way to school when I walked there, and people were nodding their heads in approval, watching me walk by. Roseanne and I remained friends after the image consulting session.

I started working out with a personal trainer whom Roseanne connected me with. This personal trainer was an actress who eventually moved out of NYC to LA and became very successful in producing meaningful films, especially around mental health. Even while she was working as a personal trainer, she was very successful and had a top-tier clientele. Some of her clientele included well-acclaimed models who represented prominent brands.

As I got into better shape, I got a set of professional photos taken. The photographer worked with Roseanne, and he did an incredible job with her photos. Roseanne connected me to the photographer, and he, in turn, did a stunning job with me. The photographer brought a hair and makeup artist along, and they helped me pick out outfits for different looks. I had my hair styled differently, and my makeup was done differently for certain looks. We started at the rooftop of my building, which had chess pieces as decorations on a chess-patterned floor. I took a photo holding a chess piece, wearing a dress and boots with some jewelry.

I then changed into a blazer, shirt, scarf, and pencil skirt and sat down for a professional photo outdoors on the rooftop. I had another outfit change and took a photo indoors on the top floor with me sitting in a chair adjacent to a bookcase on the wall. This emulated a photo seen in a law office of an attorney near legal books. My favorite was when I got dressed in a red sweater dress and brown boots. We went to the Brooklyn Bridge, and I got a photo walking across the bridge.

I was blown away when I saw the photo outcomes, and for the first time in a long time, I felt like I was beautiful. The photo shoot only brought out what was beautiful all along and how beauty could continue to shine through the more I took care of myself inside out.

OPENING UP

Another thing I started to do differently was allow myself to open up to those whom I considered friends, namely Maya, about everything I had been going through behind the scenes with my mental health crumbles, drinking to escape, etc. Maya was so supportive and understanding of me, and she was appreciative I confided in her.

She shared some of her own personal stories of how she felt similarly, feeling like she was trying to learn about herself and, too, feeling rejected and othered at times.

"Sonia, I get what you are saying. I have felt like you many times before, and I can relate to you."

"This means so much to me, Maya."

"I always craved companionship in many ways when I was living in Chicago. I wasn't happy with who I was when I was there, Sonia. I felt like I didn't know how to enjoy my own company because I didn't really know who I was. It was not until I moved out here that I started to learn more about myself. It's challenging, though, too, because it can be very lonely, and I get how you feel about watching everyone else in the dating world. It's not easy," said Maya.

"I get it," I replied, feeling relieved that someone understood me.

"Sonia, if you are ever feeling that low again, please feel free to reach out to me. You don't have to go find random doormen to find support, especially in the wee hours of the morning!"

We both laughed!

Maya and I continued to have fun together. We went to a musical and went skydiving. The skydiving just happened randomly when I happened to run into Maya and her friends on the sidewalk. Maya was like, "We are going skydiving soon. Do you want to join us?"

Out of impulse, I said yes. After all, I was still in a depressive funk, so I thought jumping out of a plane (this time a legit thrill activity, no suicide cry, fake attempt) would help get me out of it.

When you get thrown out of a plane and do flips in the air at the initial outset, it can make you first and foremost question your choices, as in, what in the living heck did I just do? Moreover, it also helps you appreciate life. I appreciated the thrill and exhilaration and the fact that there are good things to life when one chooses adventure over comfort.

By opening up to Maya, I came to learn that sometimes it is okay to unload and confide in trusting friends. Not everybody can go through everything alone all the time.

WORKING ON WALL STREET AND A WAKE-UP CALL FOR A LIFE REDIRECTION

Throughout my healing journey during the time I worked with Dr. Forrester, I put myself out there and gave dating another chance. I used a blind date service where the company matches you with people in their pool for first dates. No information about the person was given, and you weren't given that person's number. The only information you were given was the date, time, and place of where you were going to meet. You were then given a photo of the person's face so you knew who to look for at the place.

The blind dates I went on were left at just that: one date. I went on several first dates, but it never really turned into anything. There were not many people left in the pool thereafter. I never received any feedback. I spoke with Dr. Forrester about what was going on with the dating experiences.

"Sonia, here is the thing: There are guys who will see a beautiful photo of you. Then, perhaps there are things you are doing that make them question, 'What in the heck is happening?' This isn't to say that this is your fault, but guys know when a woman isn't experienced. This can be a turnoff to some men."

"I get that."

"Good thing is that at least you are practicing. Now, are you able to get any feedback from when you went out on a date?"

"I don't get feedback."

"Why don't you ask the agency?"

"Okay."

I asked for feedback. They didn't say much except that the person wasn't interested after the first date.

I shared what I received with Dr. Forrester. She shared with me an unfortunate piece of news: "Sonia, many men don't want to date a woman who is on the spectrum. You may want to look elsewhere to perhaps try to find dates. This means you may want to look into the autistic community to find someone."

"Oh," I responded.

"Well, let's think about this, Sonia. What would it look like if you could just be your full self and not have to think about some of the quirks you have? What if you didn't have to think about sensitivity and you had somebody who would take things slowly with you? What if you could be with someone who could potentially be less judgmental about you?"

"I can understand that point of view," I replied.

"I know that you mentioned before how you go out with your friends, and it has been a routine that guys approach your friends to chat. Another thing to look into is perhaps looking at friends who might be a little lower on the autism spectrum or less attractive than you. Think about it like this: back in middle school, girls would be vouching for the cute eighth-grade guys. The eighth graders would pick the girls who were in seventh grade if they were to go younger than sixth grade. Point being, if you hang out with people who are lower on the autism spectrum or maybe even less attractive than you, you may not always feel like you have something to live up to when you are around other women."

That conversation, in and of itself, didn't sit well with me. I felt there was nothing else more to do at that point, so I took a break from therapy in the spring of 2012 to just focus on myself and my LL.M. I still had fun with friends and continued with my exercise regime.

The friends who were being referenced included friends I made in the LL.M. program as I continued to work on myself. Susan and I had a falling out. Marisol and I met after the LL.M. program started. She was good friends with someone else who was in my classes. Marisol was a big ball of energy and was always up for having fun. It was like her free-spirited energy and persona were written deep into her DNA.

Susan was giving Marisol an attitude. A big blow-up came about when Marisol was trying to make conversation with Susan, and she mispronounced Susan's boyfriend's job title. Susan threw a tantrum about it and left the party with her boyfriend not too long after. With that left the friendship, which I can look back and say was for the best. If someone has the guts to mistreat you at your own event that you were courteous enough to invite them to be at, that person is not a good person for you. It hurt at the time, but I am grateful today.

Apart from Marisol, whom I am still in touch with, I made good friends with Jimmy, who was in my cohort in the LL.M. program. He was one of the first people I met during orientation.

Jimmy and I had a lot in common: we both enjoyed watching football, we grew up in the Midwest, and we had 'similar goals' career-wise. Jimmy had a passion to work on Wall Street, and I thought I wanted to do the same. It became evident that Jimmy had a serious girlfriend at the time, and they were living together. Jimmy and I still hung out as great friends and celebrated when we found out we passed the NY Bar exam, and we celebrated birthdays together.

Jimmy and I had classes together, and Jimmy was able to pick up on some of the material a bit quicker than I was, so he helped me understand some concepts. Towards the end of the LL.M. program, Jimmy ended up getting a job at an investment bank on Wall Street. He introduced me to the recruiter, who, in turn, interviewed me. I found out I landed the job right before Christmas Day in 2012. I celebrated New Year's Eve, with my start date of working on Wall Street being the first week of January 2013.

The excitement was legitimate at first. I was excited to learn something new, and I was excited about the idea of having my first real big-girl job. The first day of work was more of me getting trained on the procedures of overlooking completed paperwork for our clients to ensure they were in compliance with the Commodity Futures Trading Commission (CFTC).

If they were in compliance, all was well to go. If not, we would have to send it back to the sales team and have the clients resubmit with corrected errors. My first week on the job was nothing but excitement and eagerness to work and learn.

The excitement wore off rather quickly because it felt like the same redundant behind-the-scenes task. The other issue with compliance work was that people got let go easily once their contract was up. I was always hired on a contractual basis and was an independent contractor. The firing of people was often brutal in the sense that they only gave you a week's notice before you were let go.

I had other compliance jobs at investment banks, but ultimately, something felt lacking through it all. One thing I feared the most was the prospect of having to leave NYC. I worked so hard to gain my independence despite navigating unstable terrain in a maze where I felt my ankle could be severely twisted at any moment with the wrong step. I tried one very last straw, and that was trying to open my own practice doing special education law.

Jimmy had a connection to a person who rents office spaces in lower Manhattan, and he passed on the referral. I rented out a cubicle, and I figured it was a great starting point to have until my clientele base could grow. It was very stressful to network and build a clientele base. Safe to say, I didn't last in it for too long because I just wasn't able to pull through.

There was one conversation that gave me the ignition to finally just close the chapter on the legal field. I received a message from a lady who said she wanted to work with me. We scheduled to meet over lunch at a restaurant in the East Village.

The lady and her husband asked me questions about my outreach and where I was targeting. I told her that I had just started out in private practice, I was educating myself, and I had attended special education law conferences. I shared about having attended networking events.

She said something followed by a question in true New York fashion. "There are so many established attorneys who do what you do, and they have been practicing in this area of law for years. *Who are you?*"

She was right. To this day, I give gratitude to this lady for finally helping me see clearly the path forward and what was best for my life. However, I didn't just start changing direction in the maze to a clearer path right away. Fear still covered me like a never-ending blanket. My biggest fears were disappointing my parents and having to leave NYC.

THERAPY WITH DR. FLETCHER AND A CAREER CHANGE

I decided to go back to therapy on two things: 1. Fear of taking the next step career-wise, and 2. Anxiety over going to a family wedding.

I had my first meeting with Dr. Fletcher during my lunch break at work. Dr. Fletcher is a British Indian who grew up in a suburb outside of London. She was aware from a cultural standpoint of the stress of attending family weddings, especially when you are a female who is still single at a certain age.

One of the first things Dr. Fletcher said to me on the initial phone consultation was, "I can empathize with the anxiety you are feeling about going to a family wedding. It's all about being married in Indian culture."

"Yes. I haven't had the best of luck with dating or finding anybody. People in my family aren't shy about making comments about my singlehood."

"That is all due to insecurity and fear. I had the same issue."

That conversation was enough to get me sold to go see her for a first session.

Dr. Fletcher was trained in psychoanalysis. Through her training, she was able to really dig deep into past trauma. One blessing that came out through the work we were doing was my ability to become more honest and introspective with myself. I made some new friends when I moved to a different neighborhood in Manhattan during the time I was working at what would be my last job in an investment bank. Right next to my apartment was a local bar and bistro that became like the infamous *Cheers bar.*

I happened to meet some of whom became another group of very great friends when I stopped at the bar on my way home. I had just gotten poured on and was completely oblivious to the fact that it was going to rain that afternoon. Hence, I didn't have an umbrella and appeared as if I had just taken a shower in work clothes by the time I got to the bar.

I was asked to move down by someone so that he and his friends, who would become my friends, could all have a seat. The bar and bistro would end up becoming one of my go-to places and would serve as my spot of comfort.

As I became more introspective and started listening to myself, I started confiding in friends I made at various places like the bar and bistro and an Indian restaurant I was introduced to and started frequenting.

My friends were encouraging me to follow my passion. In fact, the friends I made started treating me, in some ways, like I was their therapist. I bonded with two girls who ended up being my closest friends out of the bar and bistro by sharing our respective vulnerabilities. My friends, Leann and Leah, were regulars at the bar and bistro. Leann worked a job close by the neighborhood, so that would sometimes be her after-work and even lunch spot. Leah worked at the bar and bistro. Leah was an avid runner, and she encouraged me to partake in my first half marathon in 2015.

Leann and Leah loved how I was never judgmental, and I let them talk through things. They felt safe confiding their deepest secrets with me as they were navigating their own journeys with relationships and life. This wasn't the first time this happened where people shared their vulnerabilities with me.

One memory stands out from when I was attending Ingham Law School. I went to a hairdresser whose salon was located in the nearby shopping mall complex. While she was working on my hair, she told me of how she just left an abusive relationship. The hairdresser started discussing what she underwent in the relationship. Even though I felt devastated for her, I felt honored that she trusted me enough to open up about something as personal as that.

The most support I received in changing careers came from my friends. Jimmy moved back to Ohio because he was working through some personal issues. Marisol moved back to Texas upon graduating with her J.D. and LL.M. She decided she wanted to work for herself and open her own practice. Marisol had a lot of connections back in her hometown, so she had a lot of prospective clients awaiting her services.

Another friend who moved was Roseanne, the one who gave me the makeover. She moved to Florida to try to set up her organizing business. Roseanne started dating someone, and they decided they wanted a change to something a little slower-paced but more manageable.

Roseanne joined a networking group, and she invited me to fly down to speak about the autism spectrum at the networking lunch. I enjoyed speaking about the symptomatology of the autism spectrum and, more particularly, how it comes across in females on the autism spectrum.

Some people in the audience spoke to me after lunch, and people were moved by the presentation because it hit close to home for them and their families. This speaking experience helped me gain my spark back for the love I have for public speaking, particularly on topics I enjoy.

Even though people were encouraging my career change, the fears I had, as stated earlier, about disappointing my parents and having to leave NYC kept me prisoner. I started binge eating as a way to cope with my feelings. It started by visiting an Indian restaurant on the Upper West Side. It was one of those things that crept on me slowly, and I started noticing the binging getting knee-deep when I was transitioning between leaving compliance and starting my own law firm.

Going to the Indian restaurant served two purposes: 1. I made friends with the workers at the restaurant from sitting at the bar, and 2. I knew I would get good food at the place. It wasn't long before I got addicted to the food.

My usual order was one naan (Indian bread), rice, paneer tikka (a creamy tomato sauce with cheese cubes), and a side of yogurt. It is not uncommon for yogurt to be eaten with Indian dishes. Let's also not forget the wine. The restaurant had a great wine selection. I would easily have up to four glasses of Pinot Noir.

At times, I would go to the nearby frozen yogurt place that was right down the street and get a dessert. As if the food and drinks at the Indian restaurant weren't enough, right?!

Furthermore, all the food and wine in the world wouldn't address the underlying fear. The only way to face the fear was to be confident in my decisions to take onus over my life and trust myself that I was making the right choices for me.

I tried my best to undo all the damage of eating by working out and running. I started getting into running in the fall of 2014. One motivation for me to get back into running was seeing posts from people talking about running the 6-mile loop in Central Park. I thought that was a stellar thing to be able to do, and I wanted to be able to do the same.

A coworker and friend recommended joining the New York Road Runners (NYRR). I joined the NYRR at a time that just happened to be a sign from God. The NYRR and Autism Speaks Team Up were partnered to do a 4-mile run for Hope in Central Park.

I kept running once that race was finished, and that was when I knew I was hooked on running with the Autism Speaks Team Up. My desire to run and my eating habits didn't match. With time, I started noticing my body getting bigger. My pant sizes started going up, and I started looking bigger in photos. I hated looking at myself due to all the weight gain.

Dr. Fletcher addressed some of the binge eating with me, but we didn't focus too much on it. We worked a lot on healing past trauma wounds, and we worked on figuring out ways for me to heal some of those wounds.

Dr. Fletcher noticed my self-esteem wasn't that great, but she didn't feel it was necessary to address that aspect more. She did, at times, compliment me and praise me, but those weren't enough in terms of self-esteem-building skills and tools I could've learned. However, I appreciated and admired how she went deeper to help me understand how it came to be and why I had such a struggle to fully embrace and love myself. I was always seen as the problem and believed all the negativity about myself because that was my foundation from the very beginning. It also cut into the fear I had about being confident to go along with a decision I would make for myself because I was never encouraged or taught that I was smart enough or knew what was best for me to make decisions.

It was not until I started touring schools for their therapy programs that I finally gained the courage to decide for once and for all to make the change. My decision to become a therapist solidified when I gave a speech at an Autism Conference in 2015.

I happened to get an invitation from someone whom I knew from Mrs. Gorman to be a panelist speaker. I enjoyed every moment of being on the panel and sharing some of my story. I felt this was where I needed to be, around other people in the autism community and in a profession where

I was able to help others. I was inspired by other individuals on the autism spectrum who followed their own dreams and pursued their passions without hesitation or caring about what others thought. Watching them and hearing their stories taught me not to be afraid anymore.

I was met with resistance, more so from my father, once I announced I was leaving the legal field. This was to be expected in all fairness.

"Don't you know what you are doing to yourself? You are going from being a lawyer with great prestige to becoming a therapist?" inquired Dad in a sardonic manner.

"There is nothing wrong with becoming a psychotherapist."

"You are making a huge mistake. I have been telling you to read and write legal articles."

"I don't want to be a lawyer."

"I don't know what got into you or who misguided you."

"This is my life. I have to live with my own decisions."

"Therapists make very little money as compared to attorneys. Up to you," he quipped.

Even though therapists may not don't make as much money as lawyers, the truth was that the degree stopped feeding me ever since I left working in compliance. I learned to invest in the stock market once I was removed from compliance as a way to earn additional income as a backup.

My father taught me a lot about the market, and he was and is very talented in investing. I, too, had a natural talent to learn about investing in the market, and I still continue to thrive in that for my own personal gains.

I discussed the conversation I had with my father and Dr. Fletcher. She told me, "Sonia, being a psychotherapist is a very respectable profession in and of itself. I had a lot of people who gave me a high level of respect. However, at the end of the day, Sonia, titles are just titles. It only shows what you do for a living, and it is not indicative of who you are as a person."

"I agree", I stated. "I feel I am better suited to be a therapist. I feel I have the personality for it, too."

"It makes sense as to why you would want to help people," said Dr. Fletcher, empathically. "You have been through so much in your life that made you the compassionate and beautiful person that you are."

"Thank you for telling me that," I responded.

I started studying for the GRE (graduate entrance exam), and I took live courses once a week. I ended up hiring a tutor to give me extra help. There was a weekend when I flew home and visited Dr. Patel and was prescribed medication to help me concentrate better on the GRE. I was never a good standardized examination taker, and I couldn't focus in timed settings well at all. It takes me a minute or two to comprehend what is being asked.

While I was taking the medications, I was getting chest pains. It was yet another wake-up call and reinforcement about the importance to stop binge eating and live in the purpose that was designed for my life. I never went to the doctor to get my heart checked, and I was just lucky I survived and got better. However, I implore anybody who has issues with binge eating and has chest pains to please go to the doctor.

I also had to get a neuropsychological exam for extended-time accommodations on the GRE. Of the people we could find to get an examination from, I ended up seeing Dr. Shah's husband.

This wasn't the first time I had seen Dr. Shah and her husband since being her former client. I had to see them for a neuropsychological exam for the bar examination's extended-time accommodation. Dr. Shah and I caught up briefly back in 2010 while I was waiting to get the test started for accommodations for the bar exam. She was in shock that I graduated from Forest Ridge High School.

"You went to school in India, right?" she asked.

"No, I continued school at Forest Ridge."

"Maybe you didn't like it there and came back?"

"I never went to school in India. I graduated with very good grades and a great GPA. I graduated from law school and am preparing for the bar exam."

"Well, you really have come a long way," she said with a face that showed she was in disbelief.

I wonder where Dr. Shah came up with the idea that I went to school in India. Maybe it was a rumor someone made up about me, and she was quick to believe it, as she believed all things negative people said about me. Maybe she made the rumor up herself. Irrespective of how such a rumor was spread, Dr. Shah probably wanted to believe I was a failure because someone else's downfall is validating to those who are insecure and unhappy with themselves. I didn't realize this until I had time to reflect and process the conversation and what transpired. Despite what Dr. Shah may have wanted to believe about me being a 'failure,' she couldn't have been more wrong!! Remember, the coat is purple!

As for Dr. Shah's husband, he made some very ignorant comments about autism spectrum disorder when I saw him for testing for accommodations for the GRE. "Sonia, you can't have autism. People with autism *don't look like you.*"

Yes, these are the words of somebody who also has a Ph.D. in clinical psychology. Nothing screams '*pathetic*' louder.

Sure enough, when he administered the battery of examinations, one of the examinations showed I was on the autism spectrum. People can have PhDs and high-level degrees all they want, but it's the open-mindedness and willingness to learn without making snap judgments that give a real education.

Chapter 26

A NEW LIFE BEGINS.
LET'S CELEBRATE THIS REBIRTH!

LEAVING NEW YORK CITY

April 2016 was the month that I decided I would move back to Chicago. My lease was up in April, and in the time between, I had taken the GRE. I came to find out that it wasn't needed for the program I had gotten accepted into. I got accepted into a graduate clinical mental health program in downtown Chicago. I was so excited, and it felt like a huge ton of bricks were lifted from my shoulders.

Before I left New York, I took advantage of what the city had to offer to the fullest. I continued to hang out at times with friends. I still frequented the Indian restaurant, but I started gradually pulling back on how often I went there. I hired a personal trainer during the time of my transition when I tried to open up a private practice, and I used the personal trainer to help me train for the last half marathon I would do as an *NYC resident.*

The trainer helped me with a lot of strength training, and we did some intense cardio bursts during our sessions. I was also put on a run training plan using a running app. I started to make some changes to my diet, but it was not enough to see a significant body change. I still had bad eating habits that needed to be fixed.

I did my first official long-distance race with Autism Speaks Team Up for the NYC half marathon in March 2016. This would've been my third half marathon to that point, but the prior half marathons were ones I ran individually without going through a charity. The NYC half was where I did the best thus far in terms of finish times. Before I left NYC, I threw a going away party with my two different groups of friends: one group was from the bar and bistro, and the other was Maya's group. We had a karaoke party in a rented-out karaoke room. We all went out afterward to a bar.

Leann, my friend from the bar and bistro, organized a going-away brunch for me. I got emotional as Leann and Leah, another friend from the bar and bistro, gave 'speeches' about me.

Leann said, "Sonia is the type of person who would do anything for anybody. In all my time knowing Sonia, she never once judged me for the choices I made."

Leah spoke after Leann and also said something emotional and profound: "Sonia if we didn't love you, we wouldn't be here today. You have such a wonderful soul about you. I pray to God and the Universe that you find someone who sees how truly special you are. I pray that you find a person who will know how to love you."

What was said to me was another shock to my system because it wasn't something I had heard about myself any other day. Even though it was a shock to the system, what was being said was a testament to the hard work I invested in myself. It just took the right kind of people to see through it, and it took the right people to appreciate one another's journeys through life.

The night before my flight back to Chicago, I had dinner with Maya and other friends. We ate at a popular Mexican restaurant near where I used to live when I lived on Wall Street. Everybody at dinner was excited for my next chapter, even though everybody was sad to see me leave. After dinner, I walked around my old neighborhood and took photos of the places I lived when I lived at two different apartments on Wall Street. I took a photo of my then apartment, and I made a collage of the places.

Saying 'goodbyes' was not the easiest. One of the hardest goodbyes I had to say was to Dr. Fletcher. She helped me realize the important things: *I wasn't the problem. It wasn't my fault. I was in a situation where I was set up to fail, but I, myself, wasn't the failure. Even though I engaged in 'attention-seeking behaviors,' it was out of a basic human emotion to want to feel connected and not feel like a reject; needless to say, treated like a bag of trash. I also had the ability to see what was best for me.* So, instead of being berated for my behaviors like I was by the school district and Dr. Shah and judged harshly from Dr. Grey, I should've been treated with more empathy and compassion.

MENTAL HEALTH PROGRAM AND MARATHONING

The move back to Chicago was anything but easy. So many questions were running through my mind on the flight back to Chicago. Am I still a lawyer even though I left the profession? Am I considered a New Yorker even though I will no longer be living there, even though I thought that was a place I would make a permanent home? Am I going to make good friends this time back in Chicago? How will my life look? What is in my future? Will I find love? Will the family friends I visited on trips back to Chicago be there for me in the long run? It all felt so filling, but the voids were clear as day.

I was a wreck, emotionally, upon the move back. My anxiety was sky-high because it was too much change all at once. I would walk around my neighborhood and pass by local restaurants and bars, and I would automatically start tearing up. I had to remind myself that it would all be okay, eventually. The one thing that kept me motivated: I was running the Bank of America Chicago Marathon for the very first time in October 2016 for the Autism Speaks Team Up.

THE CLINICAL MENTAL HEALTH PROGRAM AND LIFE'S EDUCATION OF HUMAN BEHAVIOR

My clinical mental health program started at the beginning of September 2016. For the first time ever in my whole years of life, school finally felt like a fit! It's like when you are shoe shopping and fall in love with an ideal shoe that not only feels right on your feet but is everything magical that you could walk in to feel your beautiful, confident, and sexy best. I loved the coursework, and the vast majority of my classmates were pleasant people to be around. I ended up making a few friends in the program, but most importantly, *I connected* to the material I was studying and finally *saw a future for myself.* It was a future that was sustainable and something I was able to live up to due to the love I had for helping others. After all, I didn't go through all that I had been through for nothing.

While I was acclimating to the program, I was also 'training' for the Chicago Marathon. I was at my heaviest weight, embarrassingly close to 200 lbs. Towards the end of my stay in NYC, I was careless and just ate whatever, whenever. I started working out with a personal trainer that my parents hired for me straight away. However, my bad eating habits didn't cease to exist. My energy was drained from being overweight, and I hadn't the first clue about marathon training apart from the schedule I received from a running organization I joined.

My personal trainer eventually started taking me on runs because I needed that additional support. He was a naturally faster runner, and he had completed a marathon before. He was able to help me navigate the ropes to distance running, but nothing was going to help me if I was as overweight as I was and not getting proper adequate nutrition in a way that would fuel performance. I also needed to run and walk using shorter intervals for each as a way to begin this long-distance journey instead of running for a full mile with only a one-minute walk break in between.

Apart from trying to fit in my marathon training, I was trying to navigate the so-called 'friendships' in Chicago. I had reconnected with some 'friends' and met others through those 'friends' while I was still in NYC.

Nidhi, the girl who comforted me when I was on the painfully looking tile floor that screamed "remodel!" during a cultural party back in sixth grade, and I became friends on social media. We somehow connected rather quickly. She and I bonded over our shared vulnerabilities, and we had a lot more in common in many ways. We struggled in our own ways with friendships. Nidhi was a very attractive person, so she didn't have issues with having men drawn to her.

I met her for the first time in ages back in 2012 during a trip to visit my parents. Throughout our friendship, I learned a lot from her about guys and relationships. I got to ask questions in ways that seemed safe, such as what it is like to be intimate with someone. Nidhi never judged me, unlike some men, who have before about me not being very experienced in the romantic department or with intimacy. In comparison, women seemed a bit gentler and more understanding about my lack of experiences when topics came up. I would be amiss if I didn't mention that there are women out there who gloat at someone else's lack of experience with men and are proud to be the *pick-me* ladies.

Nidhi played a major role in emotionally supporting my decision to change careers at the time I struggled within myself to move forward.

She said one thing that I will always remember, "You are not stuck."

In turn, I was supportive and a listening ear for her when she was going through things. Nidhi and I used to do fun things together, ranging from restaurants to museums to just roaming different neighborhoods and seeing the shops. We were both creative in our own ways: Nidhi was a good artist and singer and knew how to express herself in creative ways. I was still discovering my talents, and with time, apart from running. I discovered writing and that quirky jokes seemed to remain, despite years passing when I hadn't pursued comedy.

I celebrated Nidhi's marriage and the birth of her children. We celebrated her new home, which was lovely! She moved to the outskirts of Chicago. We made sure we celebrated each other's birthdays, as we both understood how birthdays can be a trigger for discomfort and sadness. With time, things started to change in the friendship. Nidhi started going through some hard times. I did my best to be present and show up for her, and I was diligent in how I checked in on her. As she was going through things, the clinical mental health program also increased in how busy it started to become.

It was challenging at first to juggle everything from fitness to the graduate program to socializing. The friendship I had with Nidhi started to become toxic after I was accused of no longer being 'a good friend.' The text surprisingly came out of nowhere after I organized for people to get together at a restaurant for a study break to eat a good and healthy brunch. Nidhi, at first, appreciated the invite. At the time before the brunch, I was working at two different internship site locations, putting together final projects, writing final papers, and studying for two separate exams. First came the licensure exam, and then, not too long after, was the graduate exit exam.

Nidhi was unable to make the brunch. That Monday morning, I got a text asking what had happened to the friendship. I told her what all had been happening with school, with my internship, and with my exams. I was hoping she would understand what all I was going through. The message wasn't received well.

"I guess we aren't friends anymore. I never thought you would be like this," texted Nidhi.

"I explained to you what all I had going on with school, internships, and exams," I said nervously because I hate confrontation. I had to stand up for myself here, though.

"And, like I didn't?! We all have stuff," Nidhi texted.

"I had to do what was best for me," I responded.

"I am going to delete you off my social media. Your excuse about staying local was bullshit because you know I am in the city all the time. I am going to delete you from my social media. This is not a friendship. Best of luck," texted Nidhi.

As much as it was a painful falling out, it's a life lesson that not all friendships are meant to last. Sometimes, the people who call you their best friend today become a stranger tomorrow. Sad how the world works at times! However, on my end, I should've been more communicative when I had become distant as to what all I had going on. That could've set the foundation up front. But, a real friend would try to understand when someone has a lot on their plate and support the friend through that process.

I met friends in other places, such as neighborhood restaurants and bars, running groups, and networking events.

With time, this rang true when I was in NYC, too; I was never good at having a core 'group' per se, but rather individual friends here and there. I was able to make other friends. Two such friends I met and became super close with were Michelle and Alyssa from the neighborhood. I met Michelle at a neighborhood bar, and we became close friends over time. I met Alyssa at a different neighborhood bar.

I was introduced to networking groups and gatherings by Michelle, and I met some more amazing people through those. There was a club membership for this particular networking group on the top floor of a building right in the heart of the city. The views were breathtaking.

Michelle and I loved having in-depth conversations about psychology and current events. We used to have fun going to different places.

Michelle was a good hostess and used to host fun gatherings. She was avid in attending Autism Speaks events in Chicago and educated others about the autism spectrum. She was the first friend who ever asked me to one day come along with my family to the Hindu Temple the next time we were to go. Michelle expressed interest in wanting to learn more about it.

During the pandemic, Michelle decided that it was time to follow her passion. Michelle expressed at various times that she wanted to open a chain of bars and restaurants. Now, we speak every once in a while through text messages. Michelle always apologizes for not being able to speak much due to the immense pressure to keep up with the bar and restaurant.

The other friend, Alyssa, and I used to get together at times to eat lunch, grab dinner, and go to museums. Alyssa was also a therapist. I enjoyed being around her, and I gravitated toward her positive energy. Alyssa ended up meeting someone while she was in graduate school. They dated for at least two years before things started getting very serious. Alyssa ended up getting married and moving to a northern suburb well over an hour away from the city.

I visited her a couple of times when she moved. The downtown area of the suburb she lives in has a lot of cute shops and good restaurants. They also have a beautiful trail that people can walk, run, and cycle on. Eventually, the visits started becoming fewer and farther between to practically non-existent once Alyssa got married. I had offered to come out to see her, but there was never any confirmation or plans set. In all fairness, Alyssa ended up opening her own practice and is a very successful therapist. I know that this wasn't done intentionally, and she was among the first to congratulate me on my podcast, On the Spectrum with Sonia. Sometimes, though, it hurts when you miss friendships.

The part of the maze that still gets confusing is whether what happens in friendships that fade and fizzle is just a part of life or is it more likely to happen when you are on the autism spectrum and people feel like they can dump you since you aren't of much value to them. I know one thing: *I am a very loyal friend, and I know that I take people very literally when they say they want to be my friend.*

This often is my stumble and downfall, as this is where the slippery rocks and stones come in that often make me lose my footing. In my opinion, it is much better to just say to someone, "I am not really feeling this friendship, or sorry I haven't been as talkative because I have something I am going through." It is much better to be upfront because it can clear up any potential misunderstandings, and people aren't left feeling bewildered. I will admit that opening up when I am going through something has been a work in progress. It was not all solved with the time I opened up to Maya. It is still a part of the maze I am navigating through.

The messages from the past still get loud at times, especially the one where I was told that it was easier to dump people on the autism spectrum because of their place on the social hierarchy.

Even though some friendships faded and fizzled, I want to acknowledge the wonderful friends that I made who stuck around for the longer haul and are currently in my life. I met some of these friends through running, events, and my building. We connect on shared interests of fitness, music, movies, museums, wine and dining, etc. I learned that the people I connect best with are people who are laid back, goal-oriented, ambitious, intelligent, and dream chasers in their own way. I connect best with people who will allow me to be *me* with all my quirks and idiosyncrasies and will not see that as a problem.

THE FIRST MARATHON AND MARTHONING'S PARALLEL TO LIFE

The Bank of America Chicago Marathon in 2016 was incredibly arduous. For one thing, I wasn't properly trained. I was rarely ever able to wake up early enough to start my runs over the weekends. I was running shorter distances and not able to keep up with the running plan. It was not until the personal trainer stepped up to help me with the running that things started to change. The distances started getting longer with the trainer, but by the time we were running together, the marathon was only a few weeks out. It wasn't good enough to get me ready for the first marathon. I stuck to the run/walk plan, where I would run a mile and walk for 10 seconds.

I set my goal to at least make the paper. Every runner who finished the marathon in the official time limit of 6 hours and 30 minutes gets their name and finish time printed in the marathon section of the Chicago Tribune. Things were starting out well on the course, but it only lasted for so long before things started to crumble. I took advice from others to take advantage of the aid stations, and I did just that. However, by mile 18, I was practically walking the rest of the marathon. I still finished the marathon, but they cut off the course. Hence, people had to finish on the sidewalks. By the time I got to the finish line, it was closed down. Thankfully, volunteers were standing on the sidewalks to hand out medals to the late finishers.

I was able to improve my marathon times once I started nipping my diet in the bud. I joined an organized running group, and my name started making the paper on the list of the many finishers. I continued to run for Autism Speaks Team Up. I got more involved with Autism organizations.

In 2019, there was an Autism Recognition Night at a hotel conference room in downtown Chicago. I was invited to speak about my personal journey with autism. I practiced a little in front of the mirror before I left for the hotel, but on the microphone, I just spoke from the heart. I received a standing ovation after that speech, and I was wonderstruck for the rest of that evening into the whole next day.

The biggest lesson learned from that night was how much value being on the autism spectrum actually has on others and how continuing to speak up and speak out can bring about positive change. Speaking up and speaking out will be received well by people who have ears open to understanding, a mind open to learning, and a heart open to love and care about autism.

With marathoning the more that I ran the marathons in not only Chicago but other cities, the more I realized how it parallels life. In a marathon, there is no other choice but to keep going if you want to cross that finish line and get the medal.

In life, I knew I had to keep going and somehow found a way to keep moving, even though life had been everything but an easy navigation of a maze. Marathoning can have its ups and downs: Sometimes, you may not finish with a goal time you set for yourself, you may not get a personal record, or the weather might just be horrendous. However, you make do with your disappointments and use them to learn for your next race.

Our disappointments and heartbreaks are always there to teach us something. Even though it's difficult to always be able to understand the reasons behind something, I believe that things happen for a greater cause. Some of the peers and professionals I encountered showed me exactly who I don't want to become like. The rejections I faced, whether it be in friendships or romantically, even though it hurt profoundly, allowed me to thrive in other areas such as career, running, this book, and podcasting.

At times, it's hard not to feel hurt about rejections and the difficulty of always feeling like you're on the outside looking in when it comes to the perceived connections people have with others that appear to be with relative ease. I always felt it was a lot of work for me to attain and keep friendships.

With regards to running, marathon training and other kinds of races taught me much about myself. Running taught me that I could become a person whom I could truly learn to love and embrace because it taught me that, as I had been throughout my life, I persevered by using the inner grit I had in me. Some repetitive patterns from the past came back with regard to running. I dreamt of making it big with running, and I wondered what it would be like to train like I wanted to become an elite runner. However, what if dreaming big about things was just a form of self-love? What if this was a way of saying, "I deserve better; I deserve more?" What if this was a way of saying, "You're meant for more?"

I got to share my story of why I run for Autism Speaks Team Up with NBC. This was yet another example that disproved the narrative of "I'm not good enough; I'm not of value, and I'm not worthy." This is what motivates me to keep on running with Autism Speaks Team Up and continue speaking up and speaking out!

The voices of those on the autism spectrum matter—their voices matter, their light matters, and their lives are valuable. They always have been and always will be.

EPILOGUE

During my line of work, I came up with self-esteem exercises for clients to use. One of which I asked them to write 26.2 things they loved about themselves. Let's conclude with my own:

26.2 Reasons Why Being on the Spectrum is Awesome.

1. I think of things in different ways and can put a unique perspective on ideas because Autism taught me to think in different ways.

2. I am intelligent, particularly on things I am passionate about because Autism allows me to absorb information about the things Autism causes me to hyper-focus on.

3. I take my passions seriously and geek out on them with immense pride.

4. I have a unique sense of humor and like to laugh at random things. After all, laughter makes life fun, right?

5. I am a late bloomer, which means I get excited by milestones in ways other people may take for granted because they may have already surpassed that milestone long ago. This helps me keep a positive outlook on life.

6. I am capable and equipped to take on life's challenges because Autism taught me to be resilient and strong.

7. I am strong mentally and physically because Autism taught me to be both in order to keep affecting change and thrive in a world that is not always welcoming of neurodivergence.

8. I am a warrior because autism taught me to fight for the life I deserve.

9. I am ambitious because Autism taught me that I can use my strengths and desires to attain the life I want.

10. I am good at helping people because Autism showed me the ugly side of humanity. Autism taught me to rise above that and show people more love and kindness.

11. I am a talented psychotherapist because Autism taught me how people like myself are needed in the field to help affect change.

12. I have a strong ability to empathize with others, even if I may not always completely understand because Autism taught me that I needed to set an example so that people could learn to one day understand me.

13. I learned to become my own best friend because Autism taught me the only person I truly had in my life was myself.

14. I am a very loyal and compassionate person to others I love and care about because Autism taught me well enough how it feels when people act otherwise.

15. I learned to embrace the word 'weird' because Autism taught me it is okay to be my unique self. Anything otherwise would be a disservice to myself, much less what I offer to the world.

16. I learned to have perseverance because Autism taught me about the power of holding onto a dream or goal and never giving up.

17. I learned to be a hard worker and educated because Autism taught me that education is power. It is through education and hard work that I was able to overcome the many obstacles the world tried to set in my way, and I was able to outshine the naysayers with grace.

18. I am grateful to the family and friends who came into my life

and stood by my side through the good, the bad, and the ugly. Autism showed me what it was like to not have people by my side, and it showed me what it was like to be all alone throughout the formative areas of my adult years. Moreover, Autism taught me what it was like to have to pick myself up when I was kicked down with nobody there to protect me.

19. I am an avid advocate for people with autism spectrum because Autism showed me what it was like to have to feel like I am screaming in a sea of people, yet nobody hears anything.

20. I learned to use my challenges as my strengths because Autism showed me that turning challenges into strengths was a way to go forth and prosper.

21. I use the pain I struggle with emotionally to better myself because Autism showed me that there is beauty on the other side of pain.

22. I learned to do introspective work because Autism taught me that there is more to me than a person walking around Earth with just a label. Autism showed me that I have strengths, and my repetitive behavioral and thinking patterns were, in fact, talents that worked in my favor. Hence, marathoning and ultra-marathoning.

23. I was allowed to treat my talents as a part-time job because Autism taught me to go full throttle with things I love.

24. I am at ease traveling places and going places alone because Autism taught me I had to love my own company and I can rise above my fears.

25. I enjoy doing things I love because Autism taught me that even though the world hasn't always been kind, I can still find ways to be happy.

26. I learned to spread the light and love of Autism because Autism showed me that it is not something to be feared but rather something to shine bright, celebrate, and be loud with.

26.2 Now, go give yourself a big hug! You've successfully, and with grace, told people who made you feel worthless, like you were nothing, who threw you to the curb once they were done with you, told you about how horrible you were, told you they adored you but now treat you like you went to your grave, and those who told you how you would amount to nothing to "screw off. Look at me now!"

Like the sun rises in the East and sets in the West, with Autism, anything is possible, including brighter and better days ahead.

ABOUT THE AUTHOR

Sonia Krishna Chand lives by the adage, "Be unique, be you." Sonia grew up in a challenging environment where she was misunderstood by society at large and by those by whom she was supposed to feel safe and protected. However, Sonia blazed her own path instead of allowing challenges to knock her down. Sonia used challenges as her building blocks to set her up for the successes she has today.

Sonia is a psychotherapist who lives in Downtown Chicago. When Sonia is not working, she is filling her time with plenty of other things, such as podcasting, running, strength training, and spending time with family and friends. Sonia is the host of the On the Spectrum with Sonia podcast, which is available on all audio platforms, including Apple and Spotify.

In addition to helping others and spreading autism awareness and acceptance, Sonia speaks on stages globally and gives valuable insight on her social media platforms. She can be contacted for media appearances and speaking engagements at sonia. krishna.chand@gmail.com and can be found on Instagram @chand_sonia.

SCAN ME

www.ingramcontent.com/pod-product-compliance
Lightning Source LLC
Chambersburg PA
CBHW051136120626
46547CB00012B/823